"If there is a teen in your life, you need this book! Elisa has written a ????, engaging, and eminently practical user's guide to your brain for adolescents. The 'brain hacks' are tried and true cognitive behavioral therapy (CBT) techniques based on decades of research, and they can lead to real change!"

> —**Beth Salcedo, MD**, immediate past president of the Anxiety and Depression Association of America, medical director at The Ross Center, and assistant clinical professor of psychiatry and behavioral sciences at The George Washington University School of Medicine and Health Sciences

"*Your Amazing Teen Brain* is a must-read for teens and the people who know and love them! Elisa provides crucial information for teens about the changes occurring in teen brains during adolescence (spoiler alert: there's a lot going on!), and she instructs the reader on how to use evidence-based CBT interventions to help manage mood and create meaning."

> —**Marci Fox, PhD**, psychologist, author of numerous books on CBT, founding fellow and certified supervisor for the Academy of Cognitive Therapy, and adjunct faculty at the Beck Institute for Cognitive Behavior Therapy

"*Your Amazing Teen Brain* is invaluable! Nebolsine shares research from the past decade about the adolescent brain, the changes and quirks that occur in the teen years, and makes it understandable and relevant for teens, parents, clinicians, and teachers. This user-friendly book is a wealth of easy-to-understand information and practical interventions that teens will embrace."

> **—Amy Wenzel PhD, ABPP**, clinical assistant professor at the University of Pennsylvania School of Medicine, adjunct faculty at the Beck Institute for Cognitive Behavior Therapy, and author/editor of fourteen books and over one hundred peer-reviewed journal articles and book chapters

"*Your Amazing Teen Brain* is a must-read for all teens—and those who live with teens! Elisa Nebolsine writes with clarity and wit, and the result is a powerful, highly engaging resource that gives teens the information they need to understand their emotions and successfully navigate through this pivotal developmental stage. By educating teens about the adolescent brain, Nebolsine empowers them to take charge of their experiences—and she gives them the tools to do this."

> **—Sherin Stahl, PhD**, faculty in the Yale Child Study Center and department of pediatrics at the Yale University School of Medicine; also in practice in in Fairfield and Woodbridge, CT

"Excellent and much-needed resource for teens! Adolescence is a challenging time, and this text provides a basic overview of what's going on in the teen brain—from intense emotion to complicated friendships. Elisa explains not only the whys of adolescence, but also provides a map of CBT skills that allow teens to navigate and even succeed during the teen years."

—**Mary K. Alvord, PhD**, psychologist, and coauthor of
Conquer Negative Thinking for Teens and *Resilience Builder Program for Children and Adolescents*

"I love this book! I want a copy for every teen and parent of a teen in my practice. CBT, the teen brain, and basic neuroscience? What else do you need? A perfect combination of important facts, strategies, and skills written in a way that appeals to adolescents."

—**Catherine McCarthy, MD**, child and adolescent psychiatrist in Washington, DC

"*Your Amazing Teen Brain* is a fantastic resource for teenagers trying to understand the incredible changes they are experiencing. It is clear that Elisa 'gets' teenagers. Everyone who reads it will benefit in some way from reading it. A true winner!"

—**Melissa Grady, PhD**, associate professor of social work at Catholic University of America, and coauthor of
Moving Beyond Assessment

the *instant* help
solutions series

Young people today need mental health resources more than ever. That's why New Harbinger created the **Instant Help Solutions Series** especially for teens. Written by leading psychologists, physicians, and professionals, these evidence-based self-help books offer practical tips and strategies for dealing with a variety of mental health issues and life challenges teens face, such as depression, anxiety, bullying, eating disorders, trauma, and self-esteem problems.

Studies have shown that young people who learn healthy coping skills early on are better able to navigate problems later in life. Engaging and easy-to-use, these books provide teens with the tools they need to thrive—at home, at school, and on into adulthood.

This series is part of the **New Harbinger Instant Help Books** imprint, founded by renowned child psychologist Lawrence Shapiro. For a complete list of books in this series, visit newharbinger.com.

your amazing teen brain

cbt & neuroscience skills to stress less, balance emotions & strengthen your growing mind

ELISA NEBOLSINE, LCSW

Instant Help Books
An Imprint of New Harbinger Publications, Inc.

Publisher's Note

This publication is designed to provide accurate and authoritative information in regard to the subject matter covered. It is sold with the understanding that the publisher is not engaged in rendering psychological, financial, legal, or other professional services. If expert assistance or counseling is needed, the services of a competent professional should be sought.

INSTANT HELP, the Clock Logo, and NEW HARBINGER are trademarks of New Harbinger Publications, Inc.

Distributed in Canada by Raincoast Books

Cover design by Amy Shoup

Acquired by Jess O'Brien

Edited by Karen Schader

Library of Congress Cataloging-in-Publication Data

Names: Nebolsine, Elisa, author.
Title: Your amazing teen brain : CBT and neuroscience skills to stress less, balance
  emotions, and strengthen your growing mind / Elisa Nebolsine.
Description: Oakland : New Harbinger Publications, 2021. | Includes bibliographical
  references.
Identifiers: LCCN 2021031222 | ISBN 9781684038046 (trade paperback)
Subjects: LCSH: Cognitive therapy for teenagers. | Adolescent psychotherapy. |
  Teenagers--Mental health.
Classification: LCC RJ505.C63 N43 2021 | DDC 618.92/891425--dc23
LC record available at https://lccn.loc.gov/2021031222

Printed in the United States of America

23 22

10 9 8 7 6 5 4 3 2

This book is dedicated to my clients. It is such a true privilege to know you, work with you, and learn from you. My work is rich, meaningful, and endlessly rewarding because it includes you.

Contents

Foreword   ix

Introduction: A User's Guide to Your Brain   1

1   Your Brain Is a Little Crazy Right Now…But That's Okay   9

2   Your Emotions Feel Bigger   25

3   CBT Can Help   45

4   Stress: The Good and the Bad   57

5   Risk, Excitement, and Drama: Your Brain Wants It All   71

6   Peers: They Matter a Lot   89

7   "School Is Your Job Right Now"   97

8   Procrastination: The Villain   109

9   Meditation and Mindfulness   125

10 Why Am I Doing All This? Finding Meaning   139

11 Telling Your Story   155

Conclusion: Your Path Forward   163

Acknowledgments   165

References   167

Foreword

Your Amazing Teen Brain is an amazing book. Written in a highly engaging style, it shows just how dynamic and powerful the teen mind is. Research has been exploding about the plasticity and changes in the adolescent brain. Cognitive behavioral therapy (CBT) is a natural fit for understanding and harnessing the power of the teen brain.

As the president of the nonprofit Beck Institute for Cognitive Behavior Therapy in Philadelphia, whose mission is to improve lives worldwide through excellence and innovation in CBT research, practice, and training, I am delighted to introduce this new tool for adolescents. It is a solid, research-based text that is engaging for teens without being "dumbed down." The author respects teen readers and writes directly to them in an honest and straightforward manner.

Elisa Nebolsine has served as an adjunct faculty at the Beck Institute for more than a decade and has been a leading practitioner of CBT. Her focus, CBT with children, adolescents, and young adults, has led her to work with clinicians, practices, and agencies across the country as both a clinical supervisor and a consultant. She brings a wealth of experience, knowledge, and creativity to her work, and these strengths are communicated in this excellent text.

The book is written for teens, but it also is a great resource for parents, educators, therapists, medical providers, and other caregivers who want to understand the dynamics of the teen brain and what they can do to help teens in need. Elisa writes clearly on the teen brain in friendship, emotion, stress, learning (and procrastination), risk, and mindfulness. She presents clear and action-oriented information, and consistently ties the research back to practical CBT strategies and techniques that readers can use to "hack" their responses.

CBT is a powerful intervention, and Elisa understands it well. This text is rich with CBT strategies that can be used by teens to manage emotions, change negative thinking, and feel better about themselves. When my father, Aaron T. Beck, MD, developed CBT in the 1970s, he recognized that clients should learn and practice skills themselves. *Your Amazing Teen Brain* provides tools to start practicing CBT today.

Your Amazing Teen Brain is a great resource for teens and adults who interact with them. I encourage you to read it and implement its very helpful, evidence-based, practical strategies.

—Judith S. Beck, PhD

Beck Institute for Cognitive Behavior
Therapy; University of Pennsylvania

Introduction:
A User's Guide to Your Brain

The teen brain is amazing. You, living with this brain, may agree or disagree with that statement. But if you step back and look at the research on your changing brain, it's hard to argue that the power of your brain, right now, in this moment, isn't awesome. Your brain is changing more now than at any other time since you were a toddler, but unlike when you were little, you can be an active part of this change. As a teen, you can make choices on which areas to strengthen and work to get rid of habits and patterns that no longer serve you well.

I am not a neuroscientist, a biologist, or a neurologist (all types of brain doctors); I am a cognitive behavioral therapist who works (and lives) with teens. This book is not a technical guide to the brain. Rather, it is a user's guide to the teen brain. This book is a tool to help you understand how your teen brain works, where its weaknesses are (so you can shore them up), and where its strengths are (so you can use them fully). The tools you will learn are based in cognitive behavioral therapy (CBT from here out), and CBT is one of the coolest ways to make changes out there. It is based on solid research, it makes sense, and it really works.

Why do you need to learn about your brain and CBT? Maybe you don't. Maybe things are perfect right now, you have no issues, and you wouldn't change one thing about your life. Except, that if all that were true, you probably wouldn't be reading this introduction right now. And even if it is true, you can still benefit from learning about your teen brain and CBT. Because there is a lot happening in that brain right now. There are reasons why some things are so hard, why you feel everything so deeply, why people delight or annoy you in more significant ways than before, and why you really want to find your place and your meaning. It all has to do with the changes your brain is making right now, in this moment.

YOUR BRAIN CAN CHANGE...AND IT IS, RIGHT NOW

Remember the first time you played a new game on your phone or tablet? You probably weren't that good. But if you kept playing, you got better. Your brain learned what it needed to do to get better because you practiced. As you practiced, you got more familiar with the game, you saw new strategies, and your score likely kept increasing.

When we learn, our brains change.

"What fires together, wires together" was first said by Donald Hebb, a scientist, in the 1940s. It's likely you've heard this quote before, but you may not know the origin. Dr. Hebb was interested in how the brain organizes and learns information. As one of his experiments, he brought home rat pups (baby rats) to live with his family. These were lab rats—not the ones creeping around sewers—but still not everyone's ideal pet.

The baby rats spent weeks with his family, and they were given free rein in his house. They could climb on everything and explore under sofas and in closets, they could play with the kids. They could do whatever they wanted. He then brought the rats back to his lab and compared them with the rats who had been stuck in cages the entire time. The free-rein rats were faster to figure out the mazes and solve problems, and they seemed to be more intelligent. This, despite similar genetics. The way they were raised made their brains different from the caged rats' brains (Jensen and Nutt 2015).

Hebb's theory, one we still use today, is that the more we think about something, explore new things, and literally use our brains, the more connections we make in our brains. This is a good thing. When our brain neurons are working (when we're thinking and learning) they "wire together"—meaning they connect and strengthen. You get better at something. As a teen, your brain is primed to make changes; it wants to learn and strengthen connections. Teen brains are more changeable than adult brains, and your brain is eager to experience the world. Which is great! But, in all its eagerness, it also is a little too reactive, it hasn't fully matured, and some of the connections and wiring are still in process. This is where CBT comes in.

CBT IS POWERFUL

CBT was developed in the fifties and sixties by a brilliant psychiatrist, Aaron T. Beck. Dr. Beck, who is still alive and working as of this writing, challenged the ideas of traditional therapy. He brought a scientific model of study to emotional and mental illness, and he used research to drive his work. This was a big deal at the time, and Dr. Beck is credited with changing the fields of psychology and psychiatry.

Dr. Beck was interested in how and why we get sick from depression, anxiety, and other diagnoses, and he explored how our thoughts (cognitive essentially means "thoughts") impact our behaviors. For example, if I think to myself, *My life is terrible, and it will never get any better,* that thought is more likely to lead to me sitting on the couch and binge-watching Netflix.

But if I can find a way to change my thoughts to something that is true but also helpful, it will also impact my behavior. This might look like: *I feel terrible right now, but this feeling is temporary. I've felt bad before, and the feeling didn't last that long. I don't feel like hanging out with friends right now, but I know that if I do spend time with them, I will likely feel better.* These revised thoughts, while still true, are more likely to push me to do something (behaviors) that will change how I feel. I think most of us have had this experience: we don't want to do something that we know is good for us, we talk ourselves into doing it, and then we wonder why we didn't just do it all along because it was so fun.

Dr. Beck, without the current knowledge of the brain and its ability to change, was recognizing that the more we do something that creates change, the more likely we are to keep doing it—in other words, neurons that fire together, wire together. If we repeatedly change our thoughts to true and helpful (from false and unhelpful), we eventually create and strengthen new neural pathways that lead us to feel better.

He went even further and looked at behavior change. If we change our thoughts, we can change our behavior, but if we change our behavior, can we change our feelings and our thoughts? Yep. We can. He also found that the beliefs we hold about the world, our innermost beliefs, influence how we think, act, and feel in situations. Dr. Beck learned that if we can change our thoughts and our behaviors, we can eventually change negative beliefs that we hold. All this occurs by our brains learning to think differently.

CBT isn't just a theory; it's practical too. Dr. Beck's work led to the development of all kinds of tricks and tools to use to hack into your brain and manage your mood. There are strategies for staying calm in moments of crisis, skills that help you boost your mood when it's getting low, and techniques for getting along with peers and feeling better.

WHY I WROTE THIS BOOK

I have been working with teens for twenty-five years. I honestly have the best job in the world. I get to spend my days with kids; help them figure out what's going on inside; learn about their hopes, desires, and beliefs; and work together with them to see what they can do to feel better. And teens are exciting to work with!

Yes, you guys have criticized my clothing, my hair, and my office decor, but it's okay because you usually were right. More importantly, you have kept me engaged and connected with the power of adolescence. I worry that in our culture we make teenagers out to all be difficult problem kids, and that we've relabeled the normal brain changes that are occurring as something that is wrong with teens.

Nothing is wrong with you. Your brain is just changing, and the changes are intense. My hope is that you can learn to harness the changes, manage them, and create a life that feels good and has meaning. Have you ever seen giant wind turbines? Often, when you're driving in a rural area, suddenly there are these huge white structures slowly rotating with the wind. That's what this book is for—for you to learn to take the energy of your age and harness it with science and CBT.

And I believe in CBT. As a person who works with kids and teens, I am very invested in using the best-researched and most effective type of intervention. Some kids need to go to formal CBT therapy and work with a clinician to learn the skills, and there's no shame in that. Some kids don't need to do formal therapy and can learn the skills on their own and practice them. That's great as well. The goal of CBT is to become your own therapist, to talk yourself through issues, and to have strategies ready to use when things get tough. Whether you learn this with a licensed therapist or on your own, CBT can help.

As I mentioned, I've been working with kids for a while, and things have changed during my decades of practice. We've learned so much more about the brain. Interestingly, CBT hasn't changed that much, but we now have a better understanding of the whys and wheres of how it works. If you need help that's bigger than offered in this book, that's okay. Ask your parents, guidance counselor, or a trusted adult for help.

One of the very best parts of my work—okay, the best part—is when kids come back after a long period of time just to let me know they're doing okay. They might be sitting in my waiting room or reach out through an email, and they remind me of the work we did together. They remember the strategies and usually have found the ones that work the best for them, use them regularly, and have disregarded the rest. They have built neural pathways and wired them together through their years of practice. The research studies tell me CBT works, but the kids I have been privileged to work with show me its lasting power.

HOW TO USE THIS BOOK

In some books you can flip to any page and find material that makes sense and is readily usable. Unfortunately, this isn't one of those books. Because the first two chapters provide the background information on the brain and CBT, they are important to read first. The chapters build on each other, and while you are certainly free to skip around, you may need to go back to reference some ideas or information.

Mostly, this book is meant to convey the information you need to know to manage your teen brain and harness its power. If it seems too simple at times, I apologize. I have the utmost respect for teens, but I often find myself making things as simple as possible for my own understanding. The more I can distill the information back to its very basic ideas, the more usable it becomes.

Thank you for reading this book. I am so appreciative of your time and attention to the material. I worked hard to make it useful and practical, and I hope it serves that role for you. If you enjoy the material, take a look at the references in the back for more ideas on what to read. Another way to learn more would be through your school—ask your guidance counselor if your school has a psychology class. The more you learn about your brain, yourself, and how you work, the more you can do to be and feel the way you choose to be.

CHAPTER 1

Your Brain Is a Little Crazy Right Now...But That's Okay

The teen brain is both incredibly vulnerable and seriously powerful. It's a tricky combination, and it explains why you have unbelievable moments of insight right alongside experiences where you act in a way you almost immediately regret. Riley, who's fifteen, can figure out the equations to solve complicated math problems, but he regularly can't find his shoes. This is the one of the complexities of life at your age—growth and chaos occurring simultaneously.

Imagine this: You're living in your dream house, and it's absolutely perfect. Everything is new and shiny; it looks just the way you want it to look. But not everything works. In fact, it's difficult to predict what will work and what won't. The lights in your room are installed, but they don't turn on. The TV and computer are brand-new, but they don't turn on either. And the garage door just doesn't open no matter how many times you click the button. The teen brain is a little like this amazing house that isn't quite ready. At this time in your life, only about 80 percent of your brain is wired for use—which doesn't sound that bad, until you start to realize that you really need that other 20 percent (Jensen and Nutt 2015).

Right now, your brain is going through a serious period of reconstruction, and you're living through it. Ultimately, the changes are going to be great, but there is challenge for you during the process of change. But if you understand the challenge and the change, there is much you can do to help yourself not only get through but actually thrive during your teen years. It may be hard to believe, or maybe you already know this, but being a teenager can be extraordinary.

First, let's look at the brain. Here's the problem: teens have excess gray matter and not enough white matter in their brains. Gray matter is the structure of your brain, the actual parts of your brain. White matter is the material that connects the gray matter and helps each section of your brain communicate with the others. Picture a floating city. All the houses, stores, and buildings are floating on water with no roads to connect them. And imagine that no one in this city can swim. What do you end up with? A city of people who can't connect with each other. But if you build bridges (or offer swimming lessons), people start to connect and move around the city.

Gray matter is like the houses and buildings of your brain, where information is stored, and white matter is the bridges, paths, and roadways that connect the gray matter. It's tough to have a city without real roads or bridges, and that's kind of what's happening in your brain right now. You've got the actual buildings, but now you need the pathways: the roads and bridges that will connect the parts.

Until you build the additional connections, things can be a little tricky. The good news is, *you* can build these pathways. You don't need to wait for them to be built for you.

Neuroplasticity is a big part of this. For most of us, "plastic" refers to something permanent or, at the very least, difficult to recycle. But for neuroscientists, plastic means changeable. When neuroscientists talk about the plasticity of the brain, they are talking about the ability of the brain to change itself.

Yes, you can literally change your brain. Right now, your brain is incredibly plastic, and capable of making real change. Relatively new research shows that you can become smarter during your teenage years. Truly. Your intelligence can actually change. A study reported in the journal *Nature* found that 33 percent of teens gain IQ points in their adolescence (Ramsden et al. 2011). You can also make changes to increase your brain power, to understand the risks of adolescence, and to live more fully and deeply. You have significant power right now.

In order to use this power, you need to understand the basics of what is going on in your brain. If you can learn what's happening, you can also learn how to harness the strengths that are developing. You have a choice. You can change your brain.

BACK TO FRONT

The human brain develops back to front. Big deal, right? Who cares how it develops? In this case, it actually does matter. The brain regions that deal with threats develop more quickly than the regions that help you think in ways that are calm and rational. This makes sense, as our first and foremost job is to stay alive. Here's the general layout of the brain:

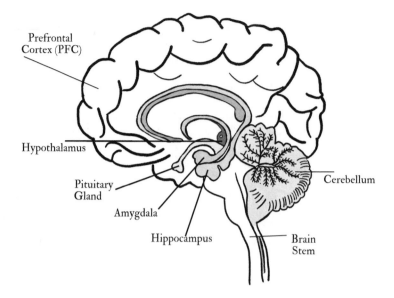

- The brain meets the spinal cord at the brain stem. The structures at the meeting point between the brain and the spinal cord are responsible for your basic life functions, such as your heart rate and breathing.

- The bump right above this area is the *cerebellum*. Cerebellum actually means "little brain" in Latin, and this little brain is a big deal. The cerebellum is all about movement. You don't think a lot when you reach for something or ride your bike, but your cerebellum is hard at work helping you stay on track.

- Moving on up to the midbrain, your brain starts to get more interesting. The *amygdala* and *hippocampus* live in the midbrain, and they are a part of something called the limbic system. These parts of the brain are all about emotion, reaction, memory, and safety. Much more to come about this part of your brain—in fact, the limbic system is a major player in this book.

- Next we look at the *prefrontal cortex* (there are actually *many* more parts to your brain, but I'm just listing the big guys here). The pre-frontal cortex, or PFC, is especially important. This is where the reasoning, logic, processing of emotion, problem solving, and other big "brainy" functions happen. It's also where we process our reactions and relationships, and think about how we fit in and matter in the world.

Back-to-front development of the brain means that the more basic and protective parts of the brain develop first. In other words, our brains develop in a way that prioritizes threat detection and reaction over problem solving. This makes sense when you think about how human life used to be thousands of years ago. At that time, it was much less important to be able to do algebra and much more important to be able to keep yourself safe. We still need to be able to detect threats and keep ourselves safe—that hasn't changed—but we also need to be able to react to situations without freaking out. And the growth and evolution of our PFC has made this possible. We don't have to just panic about nonthreatening threats because we can use our PFC to control our reactions.

SAFETY FIRST

In the ancient past, when humans all lived in the savannah and were hunted by wild animals, they needed the parts of the brain that detect threats. After all, when you're faced with a tiger, you don't really need to discuss the various ways to run away from that tiger; you just need to run.

Of course, you don't often see tigers in your life today, except perhaps in a zoo. But the part of your brain that detects threats, the amygdala, is still as active as it ever was to keep you safe when you run into things that *feel* dangerous.

The amygdala is a starring player in the drama that is adolescence. Your amygdala is the reason why you don't think about escaping a threat when you're faced with one; you just react. If this were a movie, the amygdala would be like the superhero who goes bad and starts to act kind of crazy. But just like in the movies, where someone figures out what's bothering the superhero and helps them back on the right path, we can have a happy ending. It's just going to take some knowledge and some effort.

The amygdala is referred to as a singular part of the brain, but there are actually two of them. And these structures are crucial to the human response to threat that's known as *fight, flight, or freeze*. Fight, flight, or freeze refers to an automatic process that happens when we perceive a serious threat or danger, whether that be a car racing toward you as you cross the street or a final exam that could make or break your grade. In these moments, your brain isn't interested in solving math problems or planning what to wear to school; instead, it wants to keep you safe. So the amygdala gets activated and sends out messages that you're in danger. Your heart starts beating faster, sending blood to your muscles, you take deeper breaths filling your lungs with oxygen for more energy and stamina, you may notice trembling in your hands and arms as your muscles tense to be available at a second's notice, and your digestion slows as your body focuses on the most crucial tasks at hand. All this happens without your choice; it's an automatic response by your brain to the perceived danger. But there are ways around this—ways you can hack your brain so that the way it responds to the situations are thoughtful rather than automatic. This book will teach you skills and strategies to feel more in control of your beautiful but unpredictable teenage brain.

The amygdala is fully formed at eight months in utero. You can't talk, laugh, or recognize your dog at that point in your life, but you can react to a threat. The ability to react to a threat is such an important one that our brains prioritize its development. Which is a really good thing most of the time…

Fast-forward to life in the present day, and the threats we face now aren't life-threatening in the same way as the predators of the past were. But our amygdala continues to be fully developed by the time we're born. It still wants to protect us, but unfortunately it's trying to keep us safe from things like big tests, surprise assignments, large presentations, or friends we're afraid might judge us. This means the amygdala is reacting to these events in ways that let us use less of our thinking skills (which are very needed for those tasks) and more of our reacting skills (not helpful).

Kelly, a tenth grader, took AP history to "look good" for college applications. To be clear, Kelly hates history. She finds it boring, her memory for dates and battles is not strong, and she gets very anxious about tests. Fast-forward to spring of her sophomore year, and the night before the AP test. She lies awake in bed, consumed with worry. She can't sleep; she is thinking about how much she doesn't know, what else she should have studied, and her general lack of skills and knowledge.

When she arrives at the school, and the test is finally sitting right in front of her, she can't remember anything. Zero. She just stares at the test.

Her heart is beating fast, her hands are a little shaky, and her stomach starts to hurt. Her amygdala is hard at work "protecting" her. It's interpreting her level of fear as a serious threat. It has her ready to run, fight, or stay perfectly still to avoid the threat. Unfortunately, this is exactly the opposite response to the one she needs—which is to stay calm, focus on the questions one at a time, and do her best to answer them as well as she can. As you can see, Kelly's amygdala plays a starring role in the anxious response.

And as if that weren't bad enough, your threat-detection system isn't the only thing that's making your brain reactive. There are also certain hormones being released in your brain in adolescence that interfere and steer you down paths that may not be the most helpful at this time. These chemicals stir up your brain's reactivity and make things even harder.

THE CHEMICALS ARE OFF AND RUNNING

You were born with hormones in your body that have just been hanging out waiting for puberty to kick in. Once you start puberty, those hormones switch on, and your levels increase by the thousands.

Your brain had barely seen these hormones before, and suddenly it's flooded with them. Like a hibernating bear woken up with a loud bang, they moved quickly into your body, causing all kinds of chaos.

It's pretty overwhelming, and you certainly feel the results. Think about what would happen if you gave a three-year-old a cup of espresso. The poor kid would be out of control. They'd be racing all over and they would feel great...until they didn't. Unfortunately, it's kind of the same for you. Just like a little kid surging through the ups and downs of a caffeine high, your brain is trying to figure out how to manage with this crazy influx of hormones. Unfortunately, it takes time to get used to the change, and during that time you're probably going to be more reactive, quicker to get mad, and more impulsive.

And, as if all these new hormones weren't enough, there are more changes happening in your brain chemistry. Some of the brain chemicals that helped you manage emotions and mood before puberty are temporarily on the decline. Completely unfair, but true.

Let's sum it up: at this point, we have an overreactive amygdala, tons more emotion-inducing hormones, and now we're going to add in another chemical factor—neurotransmitters.

NEUROTRANSMITTERS

Neurotransmitters are the chemicals that allow your brain's cells to talk to each other. These chemicals zip down your brain's neurons until they reach the end of the cell, at which point they literally squirt a chemical message across the *synapse* (the gap between neurons) to the neurotransmitter on the other side. They are fast moving and effective communicators in your brain.

Researcher Dean Burnett uses the following analogy to describe neurotransmitters in action. He imagines them like old-fashioned warriors on horseback. They race down pathways trying to get information to other members of their military, but they are limited by geography. The horseback warriors run into cliffs and ravines. They must therefore tie the message to an arrow and shoot the arrow across the ravine to where the next soldier waits to pick it up and move it forward (Burnett 2018).

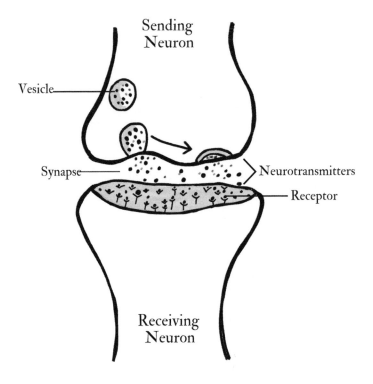

Sending Neuron

Vesicle

Synapse

Neurotransmitters

Receptor

Receiving Neuron

Dopamine, for instance, is a neurotransmitter that can be seriously helpful. It makes you feel good for doing things that are good for you. If you're thirsty and you drink water, you get a little dopamine hit. If you stick with a hard project and complete it, you get a dopamine hit. Dopamine is like your friend who cheers you on and encourages you. Of course, you also get a dopamine hit if you eat twelve doughnuts in one sitting, so the friend quality can sometimes be in question.

In puberty, your base dopamine levels are highest at the early stages, but by age seventeen they start to decline. In a 2013 program presented at Cornell University, Dr. Lawrence Steinberg said that there is no other time in your life when things will feel as good as during early to middle puberty (ages fourteen to seventeen). You have so many dopamine sensors that experiences can feel truly awesome. And, because things have the potential to feel so amazing, you seek out experiences that make you feel good. Unfortunately, these ages are also the riskiest time of your life for precisely the same reasons.

In one of the many ironies of adolescence, you get a bigger hit of dopamine for doing new things—seeking experience. What this means is that you get less reinforcement for mundane everyday tasks that you actually need to do (homework!), and you easily feel bored. But, if you do something crazy and risky, you get more dopamine rewards than at other times. Basically, you get less positive reinforcement for the necessary and more negative reinforcement for the fun (Siegel 2013). This is a bummer because your brain really wants reinforcement right now, and it seeks ways and places to feel good.

This period is risky because your brain wants to feel more positives than ever before. It pushes you to seek new and novel sensations, and you get big rushes of dopamine when you do things that feel good. At the same time, your PFC isn't really connected well (remember the floating city) so your brain has a more difficult time controlling emotions. Your brain can feel amazing because of all the dopamine sensors, but remember that when you're feeling that awesome experience, you also have to consciously think through what you're doing and make sure it makes sense. As always, easier said than done.

Dopamine is just one of the neurotransmitters in your brain. Another significant one that also is in less supply in adolescence is *serotonin*. For whatever reason, serotonin levels shrink when you go through puberty.

This is a serious problem as serotonin contributes to helping you manage anxiety, stress, and your overall mood. When serotonin levels dip, it gets much harder to avoid feeling anxious and stressed much of the time. Serotonin is lowest between ages fourteen and seventeen, but it does start to climb again as you move closer to eighteen.

Finally, *melatonin,* another neurotransmitter, does a major shift during puberty. Melatonin helps us regulate sleep, and in adolescence it suddenly causes you to stay up later. Literally. Melatonin releases in your brain up to two hours later in your teen years. You may have noticed that as you got older you had a harder time going to bed early and felt more tempted to stay up late. This isn't just you. It's a characteristic of adolescence. Thanks to melatonin levels, the teen brain undergoes a true shift to staying up later. This makes it very hard when you have to get up early for school, and it is one of the many reasons school should have a later start time for teens, but more on that another time...

So now you've got a basic background on your brain. It's oversimplified, and it won't help you much with a bio exam, but it's enough to start you out on learning what you can do to help your brain. I'll be referring back to the parts discussed and also introducing new brain parts and functions as we move forward.

Next up: we're going to look more closely at the thinking parts of the brain (the PFC) and CBT, an intervention that can help you work with your thoughts and behaviors to feel more in control. In fact, CBT can actually change your brain. Of course, any skill, thought, or behavior you practice consistently can change your brain, but CBT is a researched way of making some cool changes.

CBT, THE PFC, AND YOU

The PFC, the front part of the brain develops last (remember: back to front development). It is where we process information, plan for goals and the future, make decisions, and consciously manage our emotions. Like the cerebellum, the PFC is also a big deal. It is the part of the brain that most lets us be who we want to be. It lets us control our behaviors so we can choose to stop doing something (what scientists call inhibiting behavior) or choose to do something (plan and stay motivated). And, as a teenager, your PFC is wired only 80 percent (remember the floating city—you're still missing a lot of roads and bridges) so it isn't fully functional yet. But it's getting there.

The PFC is our thinking and logic center. Its counterpart, the *limbic system* (where the amygdala and hippocampus live) is our feeling center. When you're older, these two areas will communicate well, and it will be easier to manage emotions and work toward meaningful goals. Right now, though, they're still getting there. So, we have to find work-arounds: ways to help these two parts of your brain communicate better. And this is where CBT comes in. The goal of CBT is for you to become your own therapist; for you to have knowledge, tools, and strategies to manage your mood and emotions.

You have probably seen cartoons or TV shows depicting therapy with a person lying on a couch, and another person (the therapist) sitting behind them taking notes. This is an older type of therapy, and it's very different from CBT. I have never sat behind a teen in session, and I think it would be pretty weird for them if I did. In fact, in CBT we not only look at each other but also work together. The teen is the expert on themselves, I am the expert on the therapy, and we work in collaboration to create change.

It's actually very cool. The kid chooses the goals, I give input, and then we use research, skill-building, and knowledge about how the teen thinks, acts, and believes to create interventions.

In CBT, the most important idea is that the situation is not the problem; rather the problem comes from how we interpret the situation. For example, if I've been rejected by friends, and if I feel like this happens to me more than most people, I may be more likely to see rejection everywhere. If I met you on the street and said hi, and you walked right by without responding, I might think, *No one likes me* or *I'm so weird. Why did I even say hi?* In reality, you may not have even seen me, but I interpreted (or perceived) the situation based on things I already believe.

We form beliefs about the world around us, about other people, and about ourselves from our experiences. These beliefs are called *core beliefs,* and we tend to form them in childhood. Core beliefs influence how we see and act in the world. If we can learn about our core beliefs, we can understand how they steer us to respond to certain situations in certain ways. And if those responses actually aren't the most helpful ones in a particular situation, we can change them. CBT gives you ways to hack your brain: to understand how your brain tends to work, and change your thoughts and behaviors in ways that help you work better, so you can feel less stress and really do the things you want to do.

TAKING YOUR FIRST STEP

The first step toward making these changes is to learn to recognize emotions. I want you to be able to know how you feel in different situations. I get that this sounds simple, but it actually is hard to do. If I ask a teen how they're feeling about something, they will often say "I feel like I should be able to try harder." That's a thought, not a feeling. The feeling might be disappointed or frustrated, but I'm not sure, because all that was given was a thought. This is a normal response, and after twenty-five years of doing this work, I still have to catch myself when I start to talk about a thought instead of a feeling. So don't worry if it's still a little hard to figure out what I mean by the difference between feelings and thoughts. That's normal. It takes a while to get the hang of noticing and differentiating between them.

Your teen years are probably one of the hardest times in your life to recognize internal feelings. Your brain is changing, building, and flooded with hormones and neurochemicals, and this makes it pretty challenging to recognize what's going on inside. Everything feels big and important, and it's challenging to sort out what feeling is what. But it is absolutely possible to learn to recognize and name your emotional states. And it is absolutely necessary to learn to recognize them so that you can manage them.

This has been just the briefest of overviews of CBT, and your knowledge and skills will progress as you continue through the book. The next chapter will focus on emotions: what they are, how they work, and how you can work with them. You will learn the basic CBT understanding of emotions, how the brain amplifies emotions in adolescence, and techniques for identifying what you feel. And then, you will learn about the role of automatic thoughts and how those help us learn about ourselves and learn how to manage big emotions.

CHAPTER 2

Your Emotions Feel Bigger

You aren't imagining it. Your feelings are much bigger and much more intense, and happen quicker than before. This is an awesome gift. An overwhelming gift. You get to truly feel alive. But it is also a burden to have to feel things so deeply.

Feelings are information. It's as simple (and as complicated) as that. When you experience a feeling, your brain is interpreting your body's biochemical responses to a situation. In that way, feelings are messages from your brain and body to pay attention to what is going on inside you and around you.

Our feelings activate different parts of our brain. When you have big and intense feelings, your amygdala gets activated. The amygdala is part of your limbic system, and the limbic system is all about emotion, reaction, memory, and keeping you safe. And the amygdala is the part of the limbic system that is in charge of managing threat through the fight, flight, or freeze system. So if you experience an emotion in a *big* way, your amygdala (and the rest of the limbic system) gets turned on.

Again, your amygdala wants to keep you safe, so it tries to figure out if this feeling or emotion is signaling some type of threat. If this emotion is letting you know about a threat, the amygdala hyperfocuses on the threat to encode it into memory and protect you from this threat in the future. In other words, the more emotion is in a memory, the more likely you are to remember it. Which is why we remember the bad memories so clearly. Our brain wants us to learn from them, so high-emotion experiences get stored more deeply.

I imagine the amygdala as a little almond-shaped army general whose eyes shoot bright green lasers that lock on to the threat. The general is solely focused on this danger so that it can take in all the information about it, remember it forever, and thereby keep you safe. But as the amygdala literally laser focuses on the threat, all sorts of other things are happening in the background. The teacher may be talking about an upcoming final exam, kids might be whispering to each other, and your brain is, unfortunately, hyperfocused on the paper in front of you, missing everything else around you.

The other problem, and the bigger problem, with this hyperfocus on threats is that the amygdala and PFC can't both be working fully at the same time. If the amygdala is fully active, the PFC is not. When the amygdala gets turned on, every other part of the brain defers to its decisions and judgments; everyone follows the general's orders and does exactly what they're told. The PFC is essentially turned off until the amygdala calms down. The PFC can't do good work when it's constantly interrupted by the general shouting orders to stand down.

Right now, your amygdala general is perceiving all kinds of situations and experiences as true danger. This perception is inaccurate. Your amygdala is overreacting to situations because it is more sensitive and less connected at this age. We have to figure out a way to get more accurate information to the general. We need the general to be able to know whether something is a real threat or just feels bad in the moment. This requires the general to understand a very important fact. Feelings lie. Feelings are not always accurate.

FEELINGS LIE

I know, this sounds weird. We've all been told to "trust your gut" and "listen to your inner voice," but in reality, this doesn't always work. If you're worried about going to a party, you're not sure who is going to be there that you know, and you feel scared, is that feeling really accurate? Is there a true danger in going to the party? It's unlikely that the fear you feel is justified by a true threat to your safety, but you nonetheless feel scared.

In CBT, we challenge the idea that feelings are always accurate. In fact, we think a lot about how feelings can be misleading. One psychological test evaluates anxiety by listing a bunch of words on a paper. People who have anxiety are more likely to see words like "cancer," "murder," or "death" before people who don't have a problem with worry. The idea is that if we look for something, we find it. And when our brain is always looking for anxiety, it will find it. The same is true when we're sad. We often see and feel things as much worse or more difficult than they actually are. And when we act on those mistaken feelings, we behave in ways that are counterproductive. For instance, when we're sad, it feels better to lie on the couch in our sweatpants than it does to do schoolwork. That's also not very helpful; often, the work we haven't done piles up and becomes unmanageable. Looking at feelings realistically and factually (trying to find the evidence for them) is a crucial way to work on this skill.

There are specific ways that feelings can lie or mislead, and we call these types of ways *cognitive distortions*. Our thoughts get distorted in ways that are strikingly similar and predictable. If you google "cognitive distortions," you'll get a whole list of ways that our brains trick us into believing something is true—even when it isn't. Cognitive distortions are thinking errors, and we all make thinking errors.

Here's an example: Alex, a fifteen-year-old, gets his AP history test results, and he got a D. He thinks to himself, *I always mess up. I always get bad grades!* If we look at the facts, Alex rarely gets bad grades. In fact, he does extremely well in school. But in this moment, his thoughts have tricked him into believing this happens all the time. This type of thinking error is called an *overgeneralization.*

If Alex were to have a different thinking error, one called *mental filtering,* he would see only the bad in a situation and filter out the good. For example, Alex's teacher tells him that she wants him to represent the school for a science project, but only if he can revise his experiment a little first. Alex's first thought is not *WOW! I'm being asked to represent the school!* His first thought is *I must have done something really wrong. I have to revise my project? I messed up.* Mental filtering is when we get a lot of good information, but instead of focusing on the good, we find the small negative details and make those the focus of our attention.

Everyone makes thinking errors. Everyone. The nice thing about cognitive distortions is that they are universal. It isn't just you who has thinking errors, it isn't just teens. Every single one of us has thinking errors, and if we can learn the most common ones, we can often catch them and change them. We'll talk about automatic thoughts in later chapters, but cognitive distortions can often be a tool for understanding how thoughts and feelings can mislead us. Remember, just because something feels true doesn't mean it is true. What are the facts?

BRAIN HACK: Use a positive mood to your advantage.

Build your confidence by conquering goals when you're in a positive mood and well rested. Research shows that when we're tired or in a negative state of mind, things feel much bigger and worse than they really are. In one study, researchers found that people who were tired or negative rated hills as significantly bigger than they really were. In another study, researchers found that people who were tired felt like their backpacks were much heavier than they were (Achor 2010). Try this out yourself. When you're happy, try to do something challenging. Maybe run a mile in a certain time or read several chapters of a hard book. Then, the next time you're feeling low or are sleep deprived, try the same thing and see how it varies. From there, consider how you can change your routines so that you're doing things that are a little tougher when you're in a good mood and can handle them better.

UNDERSTANDING YOUR FEELINGS

Feelings are information. Each feeling gets processed differently, and each feeling motivates the limbic system in a different way. For example, happiness can motivate us to join in or participate, whereas anger can motivate us to stay back or lash out. Disgust serves a useful role in motivating us to stay away from something that might be dangerous or harm us, and compassion can motivate us to give comfort and support to others who need it. Emotions give information and direction, and we rely on them to move through the world. But this can be very tricky when the information they provide is incorrect because, as you now know, feelings are not always accurate.

There is a range of feelings. You can think of them as being on a scale from 1 to 10, with 10 being the very biggest the emotion you can feel and 1 the least. For instance, if a friend happens to be annoying you, and you're at a 5 on the anger scale, you might think *He is so annoying. I'm leaving. I just don't like this.* But if you're at a 10, maybe it sounds like *I'm LOSING it. I can't look at you. I can't talk to you. Get away from me!* Emotions can also feel different to different people, and different situations can increase or decrease the way we feel an emotion.

But at the end of the day, feelings are temporary. This statement is something of a mantra for me. Whenever I'm overwhelmed with sadness or negativity, I remind myself, *Feelings are temporary.* It's simple but true. Most feelings don't last that long at all. It's just that bad feelings feel like they will last forever, but just because they feel that way doesn't mean they will.

There is a concept called *habituation.* Habituation basically means that something can't continue to cause you huge emotion over time because you simply become used to it. One easy way to think about this is to imagine jumping into a freezing cold pool. If you climbed right out and then jumped back in, the water would feel just as cold the second time around and the third time and the fourth… But if you jump in and stay there awhile, and you tolerate the discomfort of the cold, in time you become used to the temperature. The water temperature doesn't change, but you habituate to the cold and it isn't as unpleasant.

This idea of habituation works for emotions as well. That is, the first time you go through a particular experience, the emotions you feel in response may be strong and overwhelming. But if you stay in that situation long enough, the feelings become easier to bear. Habituation is the process by which our brain learns, through repeated exposures, that we can tolerate emotions and experiences. We can learn to handle difficult things, but it does take effort and practice.

I know a sixteen-year-old girl named Zoe. Zoe can be fearless. She will ride any roller coaster; she has no problem climbing any and all trees (and buildings); and, despite a recent broken arm, she will mountain bike down steep trails and paths at breakneck speed. But Zoe is scared of dogs. Terrified. When she is around a dog, she continuously thinks, *It's going to bite me, I know it's going to bite me,* and she feels scared, anxious, and stressed. Her best friend has a pet dog named Jello, a brown mutt that weighs about thirty pounds, and she is afraid to go to her friend's house because of the dog.

Zoe decided to learn a technique called exposure to face her fear of dogs. Her goal was to be able to comfortably hang out at her friend's house. She started by watching videos of dogs, watching dog movies, and even going to the local dog park where she stood outside the fence and watched the dogs play. She felt fear in all these situations, but she let herself experience the fear. As Zoe was repeatedly exposed to the fear and didn't have anything bad happen to her, her brain started to unlearn the fear response to dogs in videos or behind a fence. Next, she went to her aunt's house and spent time with her aunt's ancient dog. It was not as effective as going to the dog park (the dog slept, snoring loudly, the entire time), but that's how it goes. Zoe continued to slowly expose herself to safe dogs, and soon she was ready to go to her friend's house.

When she first arrived, Jello jumped and barked at her. "He's just saying hi," explained her friend. Zoe's heart was racing, her hands were clenched, and she was breathing fast. Her thoughts focused on the danger of the dog in front of her, but she forced herself to slowly breathe in through her nose and out through her mouth. She caught her breath and began to work on changing her thoughts to calm, realistic, and helpful thoughts. Once Jello stopped jumping, she sat down with her friend and let him sniff her. It was totally scary, his face right near her, but she kept practicing deep breathing and calm thoughts, and soon she was even able to touch him. After thirty minutes, she was petting him, her heart was beating normally, and she was able to have a conversation with her friend. She wasn't thinking only about her fear.

Habituation is the process by which we unlearn fear through repeated exposures. A wise kid I know defined it as "our brain learns to reinterpret fear and learn that it really isn't scary." Exposure and habituation are some of our most powerful tools for managing emotions of anxiety and fear.

PUTTING EMOTION KNOWLEDGE INTO ACTION

You now know that emotions are information, but that information can be inaccurate. Big emotions can trick you into believing something is bigger and worse than it actually is. You also know that all feelings are temporary; they don't last forever (even if they feel like they will). And you understand that we can unlearn emotional responses by habituation. Whew. Let's take a look at how this might play out for you and see if we can make the concepts crystal clear.

Imagine you just gave a presentation in civics about the Bill of Rights. You hate giving presentations. You actively dread talking in front of other people, and you always feel nervous before and during the talk. This time, you know that your voice shook a little in the beginning, but the rest of it seemed to go okay. But, at the end, you notice some kids laughing and talking to each other. You assume they are laughing at you because you must have done something embarrassing.

You could be right. They could be laughing at you. You could also be completely wrong. They could be laughing at something completely unrelated to you. What are the facts here?

- You hate giving presentations. They make you really anxious.

- You always assume the worst about any presentations you give, but you routinely get As and Bs on presentations from your teachers. Not just one teacher, but most teachers.

- The kids who are laughing and whispering are good friends with each other. They also happen to be kids the teacher often tells to be quiet, since they're often laughing and whispering during class.

Once you have the basic facts, try asking yourself a few more questions. In this case, I would want to know:

- How many other kids are giggling and whispering?

- How many kids are giggling, whispering—and looking at you?

- How often do kids in the class giggle and whisper in general?

If you don't see anyone else, and if no one is directly looking at you, is it realistic to assume, based on the facts, that at worst two people were giggling at you, and at best, no one was? My guess is your feelings are tricking you. Anxiety is notorious for making things seem bigger and worse than they really are. If your feelings are inaccurate, how does that change how you think about the situation? Does it help to remember that this feeling is temporary and will end? And, if you were to give presentations regularly (as in every day) for a couple of weeks, what difference would that make in how you felt right now? Would you perhaps habituate to the anxiety that giving presentations causes you?

Again, anxiety—or anything you feel—isn't always accurate. You might be looking at the situations you're in in ways that are a little distorted. And how you feel is influenced by other factors, too, like whether you're well rested, whether you're eating well, exercising, and taking care of yourself, and the kind of support you have from others.

BRAIN HACK: Sleep nine hours a night.

Sleep matters for emotions. When you don't get enough sleep, your brain thinks you're in danger. It notes that you're less able to handle challenging situations, and it's ready to react quickly since your thinking won't be as clear. Your limbic system becomes even more reactive when you're tired, and it basically panics about everything. Sleep is a crucial brain hack to let you function academically, socially, and emotionally at your best, and teens need more sleep than they think. Nine hours a night makes a difference.

So now you know that feelings are information, and if you interpret your feelings and the situations that cause them more accurately, you can choose how to respond. And you can choose to respond in ways that are helpful in dealing with the situations you're facing and not so amygdala driven. Let's explore a technique you can use to put these insights into practice, called name to tame. I imagine you're rolling your eyes as you read that, but it's a legit strategy. The process of identifying, naming, a feeling is an essential part to managing it.

NAME TO TAME

The first step to managing emotions is to be able to identify what it is that you're feeling. This may sound ridiculously simple and even a little patronizing. Let me explain why this matters and how it works.

In some ways, your amygdala (and your limbic system in general) is like a toddler. You've probably seen a little kid screaming and flailing around at the store or at a relative's or friend's house. They are bright red, inconsolable and completely irrational. It's a little disconcerting to watch a full-blown toddler tantrum. It's intense, visceral, and overwhelming. And, as uncomfortable as it is to see a toddler lose it, imagine if an adult lost it this way. It would be downright scary.

Toddlers are known for their temper tantrums; it's developmentally appropriate for their age. Toddlers have very limited language. They don't have the words to say "I absolutely must have another cookie because the first one was so delicious, and I can't imagine not having a second." Instead, they feel the emotion and express it without language. It isn't pretty; all that raw emotion without language can be misunderstood and is very off-putting to those who witness it. And it also isn't very effective at getting toddlers what they want. Unfortunately, sometimes emotional experiences in adolescence can feel the same: big emotions and no words to describe them. That's when the amygdala is in charge.

Naming is a very human way of differentiating things. When we name something, we make it personal, unique, or just easier to recognize. If you were at the dog park and your pup, Scooby, was taking another dog's toy, you would probably yell "Scooby, drop it!" What would happen if you just yelled "Drop it!" out loud? I imagine a lot of confused dogs and owners would be staring back at you. It's important to name your dog so that he understands you're talking to him. The same is true for emotions. We have to name them to identify them.

None of your feelings are named Scooby (I hope), but they do all have names. Specific names that describe them. Jealousy is often called the green-eyed monster because it feels so strong and powerful. Anger is often described as fire or flame because of how quickly it can ignite and spread. The names of the emotions tell us about what we're experiencing and give us and others an idea of what the experience is like.

Emotions often arise from the limbic system. Emotions, by their nature, are intense. And while we give them simple names, they're quite complex. For instance, the anger you may feel at someone else is different from the anger you may feel toward yourself. And sometimes we may feel different, even conflicting emotions at the same time. For instance, we might feel joy when we win a game, combined with sadness or even guilt for the friend of ours who was on the losing team. Emotions can be hard to understand, and, as a result, they are often misinterpreted or misinformed. So we need to get the PFC to help us understand emotions and get a handle on why and how they have their power.

Often, the best way to do this is to put words to what you feel. Marc, a teen I know, regularly writes in a journal on his phone about what he is feeling. I encourage Marc to do this because (1) he finds it helpful and (2) I know that exploring emotions through writing (and language) is a great way to manage them. Once we bring words and language into the experience of the emotion, we can start to process and understand the emotion rather than just riding its existing wave of energy and momentum. We move out of the tantrum and into an understanding of what we're feeling and why we're feeling it.

There is no doubt that therapists love to get kids to identify their feelings, but there is real research behind the idea that naming our emotions helps to tame or manage them. Researchers at UCLA used an fMRI (a machine that shows brain responses in real time) to show the effect of labeling emotions. They showed angry faces to participants, and when participants were able to simply identify that the face was, in fact, an angry face, the amygdala had less activation (Torres and Lieberman 2018). When the amygdala, and limbic system in general, are less revved up, the PFC gets more involved and helps us respond instead of reacting. The researchers compared putting emotions into words to hitting the brakes at a yellow light. You get time to stop before moving into danger.

In another study at UCLA, researchers looked at how we overcome fear. Participants were asked to try to touch very large, very hairy, and very creepy spiders. Most people did not want to do this, and they struggled with the task. The researchers found that when the participants were able to name and describe their emotions ("I am so scared, this spider looks terrifying!") they were much more likely to be able to actually touch the spider (ew!). The act of naming our fear helps us move out of the pure emotional reaction (think temper tantrum) into a more conscious PFC-friendly state (Kircanski, Lieberman, and Craske 2012).

Naming emotions sounds easy, but, as with most things, there is effort and practice involved. The first step is to recognize what you're feeling. I don't know about you, but there are times when I've been crying and assumed I was sad. As I thought it over, however, I realized I was also angry. Tears didn't just equal one emotion, they reflected several. Learning to recognize the emotions we're feeling and name them is tricky. But the more you do it—actually pause when you're in the grip of a strong feeling and think about exactly what it is you're feeling, doing your best to be specific—the better at it you will become.

BRAIN HACK: Put feelings into words.

Language is the superpower of humans, and we can use it to understand our internal experience, even change it. The next time you're in a tough situation, or you can feel yourself struggling with some big emotion like anxiety or stress, try journaling or even writing a few sentences in the notes section of your phone. This can clarify what you're feeling, why you're feeling it, and what you might be able to do about it.

EMOTIONS ARE CONTAGIOUS

Newborn babies are usually placed in hospital nurseries while their parents sleep. You have probably seen images of this—all the babies are swaddled in blankets, they're wearing little hats, and they have identical cribs with their names on the front. In this scene as I picture it, they are all sound asleep. But what happens when one baby starts crying? The other babies usually start to cry too. This isn't unique to babies (other than the outfits and setting); emotions do have a contagious effect. Which means we need not only to know our own emotions but also to be able to recognize emotions in others.

For example, Taylor, a sixteen-year-old, told me about a time her friend Anna came up to her and started talking. "She was so mad. It was like she was yelling at me. I had no idea what I had done, and it made me so mad that she was talking to me this way for absolutely no reason." Taylor got mad at Anna. "I raised my voice right back at her, and soon we were both yelling at each other. I still didn't know why this started, but I was feeling really mad by the end."

What might have been different if Anna had approached Taylor and said, "I'm so mad. My teacher was so unfair"? Taylor most likely would have said, "I'm sorry. That's terrible. She shouldn't have treated you unfairly. What happened?"

That is what would've happened if Anna had named and described what she was feeling. Instead, Anna's anger became contagious and went back and forth between the two of them, growing bigger with each volley. Naming the anger would have most likely prevented it from spreading. In this case, this isn't a hard thing to do, but it is a little counterintuitive. Meaning it takes deliberation to notice, name, and talk about emotions. It's kind of a pain to do, but it's also a pretty simple way to reduce a lot of much bigger pain.

When we take the time to name and understand our feelings as best we can, and to carefully and thoughtfully observe the feelings of others, we actually make it easier for our brain to process both our feelings and others' feelings. Research shows that putting words to feelings (kind of like putting words to music) actually lets us handle them more effectively. The cool part here is that you don't always have to speak the words, you can also write them or even draw them. Getting the emotions into words and then getting those words out of your head can make you feel a lot better.

BRAIN HACK: Change your viewpoint.

When you or someone you know is struggling with feelings, try changing perspectives. Of course, sometimes we're not the Annas in a given situation, but the Taylors. That is, we're not the ones feeling the tough emotions; instead, we're dealing with someone else who's experiencing a tough emotion. The good news is, there are ways you can handle that too. Yale medical students who took an art appreciation class saw a 10 percent increase in their ability to spot important medical details (Achor 2010). They were able to see differently because the class taught them ways to spot small differences; it helped them change their perspectives and see things in multiple ways. The next time you're in a situation where it's hard to read the other person's emotions, try to look at in a variety of ways: from that person's point of view, from the point of view of an observer, and from the point of view of someone who was new to the school. Changing your view of the situation can cause you to see things in a new way, and maybe even spot things you hadn't seen before.

WHEN WE DON'T NAME OR TAME

Sometimes when we feel things deeply, it can seem pretty bad. The last thing we want to do is talk or write about it. We just want to move on and forget about the whole thing. I work with a lot of teens who start therapy by telling me that the only thing that helps is to avoid the feelings. Unfortunately, that doesn't work. When we ignore emotions and *internalize* them—the fancy word for stuffing emotions deep down inside of us—they just linger. They lie in wait, and the next time we feel bad about something, they come out bigger and stronger than before.

Katy, a teen with a history of depression, just hated feeling so bad all the time. She decided she was done with feeling. Of course, this isn't really possible, but she gave it her best shot. She filled all her time with activities, TV, people, noise in general. She found the negative thoughts creeping back in when she went to bed, so she started listening to podcasts to fall asleep. She did everything she could not to think about her feelings.

She thought she had the low mood beat, but she couldn't keep up the constant busyness. With no breaks at all for her thoughts to emerge, she was simply exhausted. And when she did finally break down and let the thoughts resurface, the feelings were absolutely terrible. The feelings had grown exponentially stronger as a result of being stuffed away.

My very unscientific way of thinking about this is that when we don't name or express our feelings they kind of ferment. And not the good fermenting like kombucha or cider; they ferment into something gross and smelly. We have to give them air, let them see the light, hold them close and actually feel them to give them even a chance to pass. This is hard, but not as hard as avoiding your thoughts all together...which really isn't possible.

Trying not to think about your negative thoughts and feelings is also absolutely exhausting. The avoidance, the stuffing of emotion, the constant mental activity takes a toll. In CBT, we often ask people who are trying to avoid thoughts and feelings to try not to think about a pink elephant. Can you do that now? Can you please not think about a pink elephant? Let's go even further, and can you please not think about a pink elephant wearing a light green dress and walking on the beach?

If you were able to avoid the image of the elephant, it no doubt took a lot of mental work. Most likely you, like most of us, immediately imagined the pink elephant as soon as you were told not to think about it. Not only is it supremely tiring to try not to think of something, it's often literally impossible. So let's stop trying to block out the bad thoughts and feelings, and let's let them in—but not for tea and cookies. We're going to let them in so we can understand them and work to take away their power. There are lots of different strategies for changing thoughts and feelings, and now we're going to look at how some of these work. But remember the bottom line: avoiding your feelings is not a strategy that works long term, no matter how much we love the idea.

There is something called the *cognitive loop*. It's a fancy term psychologists use that basically means our feelings impact our thoughts. I'm sure you already know this. If you're seriously sad, your thoughts are probably not going to be about how wonderful your life is, how great your family or friends are, or how good you feel. Your thoughts tend to mirror your mood—which often ends up making your moods more intense. If you're sad, your thoughts are more likely to include things like *I hate my life right now. I feel so bad. I'll always feel sad.*

Those three sentences reflect how you feel. And they also make it more likely you will continue to feel bad. The more you feel sad, and the more you think to yourself how bad everything is, the more likely you are to stay in your pajamas and not get out of bed.

Now I know I just said avoidance doesn't work, so what does work? If we want to change how we feel, we have to change either how we think about a situation—say, by looking at the situation and how we're interpreting it, and whether that's accurate, just as you did in this chapter—or how we act about it: how we respond when a given emotion arises.

BRAIN HACK: Act the way you want to feel.

When we're struggling with certain feelings but don't want to respond by avoiding things, it can sometimes be enough to simply *act* the way we wish we *felt*. This idea is similar to things you've probably already heard like "fake it till you make it." It sounds a little silly, but it actually has some real brain research behind it. In CBT we have a saying that "activation precedes motivation." Basically, this means you have to *do* something before you *want* to do it. For example, if I want to exercise more, but I never go to the gym, I have to *push* myself to go to the gym rather than wait until I feel like going. Once I get there (and this is a true example) I might end up thinking *This isn't so bad. I actually kind of like this.* Those thoughts, and the positive feelings they generate, make it easier for me to go to the gym the next day. Same thing if you're facing something kind of intimidating, like giving a presentation or having a hard conversation with a friend that you know you need to have. If you can act in a way that suggests confidence—like stepping up to the front of the class and diving into the presentation even if you're nervous, or reaching out to your friend and starting the conversation—you'll often find you're more motivated to carry on with what you're doing than you thought you were. When we act the way we want to feel, we make it more likely that we'll feel better.

EMOTIONS, THOUGHTS, AND CBT

Emotions are powerful, and they are amplified in adolescence. The next chapter explores the connection between thoughts and feelings; how we think directly impacts how we feel. Feelings and thoughts tend to be BFFs—they mirror each other. But if we can change our thoughts (it actually is possible), we can change how we feel. I'm not saying that this process is easy or simple, but it is totally possible. This chapter explained the basics of emotion: the experience, the research, and strategies for managing emotions. The next chapter does the same for thoughts. You're going to learn about how thoughts and emotions interact, and about the seriously powerful ability your brain already possesses to change how you feel by changing how you think. You'll learn how apply that insight to the situations and thoughts that most often drive your stress, and how to hack your thought patterns so you can stress less and do more.

CHAPTER 3

CBT Can Help

When my oldest daughter was little, we went for a walk in the woods. We got to a creek, and she kind of freaked out. She was scared to go across, she thought she would slip and fall, and she couldn't figure out where to put her feet to make it across the rocks. Eventually we made it over, and we soon came to an unexpected steep cliff (maybe not a cliff, but a really steep drop) that we had to scramble down, using our hands as much as our feet to make it safely. Whew! It was scary, but we were fine. We got to the bottom, kept walking, and had a great time.

On our way back, we crossed the same creek that initially had scared her so much. She didn't even hesitate to cross it—just skipped right over the rocks. When I pointed out to her how well she had done, she didn't believe it was the same creek. Of course it was, but the other, steeper and scarier, parts of our walk had changed how she viewed this creek.

This is the idea with CBT. It's not the situation, but rather how we view the situation. The creek wasn't the problem, it was her thoughts about the creek that got in the way of her crossing it. We know this because when the scary thoughts weren't present, she skipped right over it without a second glance.

THOUGHTS CAN CHANGE

What are thoughts, anyway? They can be images, words, memories, anything that goes through our mind. They're always happening in our brains. And quickly, too: scientists estimate that we have around six thousand thoughts a day (Tseng and Poppenk 2020). Your brain is seriously busy thinking—even when you don't realize you're doing it. And thoughts and thinking take a lot of energy. A full 30 percent of the calories we take in each day go to fuel our brains.

Our thoughts move through our brains at lightning speed. Imagine an entire street filled with a row of trees. Their branches are lined up, and they stretch down as far as you can see. Each branch has small baby branches coming out of both ends. Now imagine light zipping between those branches, and making a path that flies down the street, instantly connecting the branches. That's how our thoughts work in our brains. Electricity and chemicals moving at amazing speeds through our neurons.

This constant movement can make it hard to always notice and catch our thoughts; how could anyone remember six thousand thoughts in one day? We notice and remember some of our thoughts (usually those with a higher emotional content), but most are just below the surface of our awareness. We can notice them, but it takes real effort to catch them. Catching them refers to deliberately noticing them and often writing them down or recording them in some format.

There is a special type of thought we talk about in CBT called *automatic thoughts*. Automatic thoughts are evaluative thoughts that come up just below the surface of our awareness. We're always having these types of thoughts, but we don't always realize that we're having them. Usually, when we start to really make an effort to pay attention to our automatic thoughts, we can notice them and catch them.

Automatic thoughts are clues. Once we get used to noticing and catching them, we usually find patterns in the thoughts that reflect our beliefs about ourselves. So much of our brain operates unconsciously, and this noticing of automatic thoughts is a powerful tool for bringing the unconscious to the conscious mind. And by noticing these thoughts we can start to change them.

You, right now, have thoughts firing mindlessly through your brain. I do too. As these thoughts fly along our neural pathways, we're encouraging the neurons through which they travel to build and get stronger. Some of these thoughts may be helpful, but some may not. And we don't want to give free rein to the negative thoughts. The last thing we want is for the pathways on which those thoughts travel to get stronger and for them to stay automatic.

One teen I work with started tracking how often she criticized herself, and she found it was up to ten times an hour. Her automatic thoughts were sentences like *How am I so stupid?* or *I'm so useless.* She knew she had a lot of negative self-talk, but tracking these automatic thoughts was a big surprise. She had been completely unaware of how frequently she spoke to herself this way. Without meaning to, she was building paths that made it easier to tell herself all the things she most did not want to be true about herself.

All humans have a tendency to think negatively. And your brain is so emotional and reactive at this time in your life that it is especially likely to get negative. Our brains do this with the best of intentions, to keep us safe, but it is enormously unhelpful when you're a teen in a modern society and just trying to figure out how to find your place, your people, and your purpose. Still, don't despair if you find your thoughts go to the negative. It's normal. It's okay. And you can change this pattern. You can hack your brain by thinking different thoughts and wiring new neural pathways that make your thoughts in general more positive and more helpful. Let's look at how to do this.

NEGATIVE AUTOMATIC THOUGHTS IN ACTION

Jonathan worries about what other people think of him. He assumes people don't like him, and he suspects that he acts weird at school and with same-age kids in general. In history class, the kid sitting next to Jonathan turns to him and asks what he thought about the homework. Jonathan responds with a shrug and thinks, *He's just being polite. He really doesn't care what I think. Or maybe he wants to copy from me.* These thoughts make Jonathan feel isolated, uncared for, and alone. The thoughts may be accurate; they also may not be. There's no real proof either way. But by assuming they are accurate, Jonathan inadvertently hurts himself.

When we choose to believe our negative thoughts, instead of looking at the reality of the situation, it usually makes us feel worse. This is very similar to how it works with emotions. Believing our negative thoughts changes our behavior, or how we act. If Jonathan believes the worst, he doesn't really respond to the kid talking to him, and he ends up looking unfriendly and awkward. While he doesn't know for sure what the kid was thinking, there is nothing gained by assuming and believing the worst possible thoughts. In fact, by believing those thoughts, Jonathan ends up acting in a way that seems unfriendly. He behaves in ways that make his own suspicions come true.

What if Jonathan were to reframe his thoughts by changing them to realistic but slightly more positive thoughts? Instead of assuming the worst, Jonathan could think, *He's making an effort to talk to me, and I should do the same* or *Does he think I'm weird? Oh well—even if he does, I may as well be polite.* The trick to changing thoughts is to keep them believable. You don't want to make them too good (*He must think I am so cool, and he wants to hang out with me after school*) and you also don't want to make them too terrible (*He's trying to set me up to look dumb so he can laugh at me*). There is a realistic and reasonable midpoint that works.

Just like Jonathan, we all have negative thoughts. These thoughts are unwelcome intruders, and without conscious care, they zip past the PFC and right over to the amygdala, and get us agitated and reactive. It happens to everyone, but it happens more easily and more often for teens (sorry!). Take a minute to notice some of the thoughts that get in the way or make you feel worse about a situation, and write them down on a piece of paper or in the notes section of your phone.

Pick one of those thoughts and take a quick second to try reframing it. Think about these questions:

Is this thought always true?

Can I think of an alternative thought that's more accurate to the situations I find myself in? And more helpful, in terms of what I can do about those situations?

It's okay if you find it hard to reframe the thought you had in this way. We'll continue practicing this skill throughout this book.

CHANGING THOUGHTS TAKES TIME AND PRACTICE—BUT IT IS POSSIBLE

Picture a room filled with snow. The snow is deep, it goes up past your waist, and it's impossible to move around in it. You have a shovel, and you slowly start digging through the snow—not all the way, just enough to make a path to get to the other side of the room. It takes a lot of digging, but eventually you get to the other side of the room. The path still needs work so you start walking back and forth on it, and the more you walk, the more you pack down the snow. Eventually, through hard work and repetition, you have created a clean, smooth path through the snow.

This snow path is similar to how our brains make new neural pathways. Thoughts create paths. If we have been thinking one way for a long time, there is a deep grooved path for that thought. For better or worse, our brains prefer the easy, established pathway. When we start to think new thoughts, we're literally building new neural paths. This process of changing thoughts and subsequently building new paths takes time and practice, but it is 100 percent possible. The more we think the new thoughts, the better the pathway forms.

The problem is that we usually don't want to make the effort to build a new path; why bother when there's already a perfectly good one right there? It isn't easy or natural to change our thoughts. In fact, it is a deliberate and effortful act to think in a new way. We have to choose to change the thoughts, and then we have to practice the new thoughts to get them to stick.

BRAIN HACK: When you're practicing thinking new thoughts in response to situations, visualize how you want to think and behave.

When we change our thoughts, it can take some time for the new neural pathways to build and become rote. During this time when you aren't seeing the results, it can be hard to keep practicing the new thoughts. But you can hack this by visualizing the way you want the situation and your response to it to look. For example, Jonathan can imagine himself responding to the kid who was talking to him. He can create a movie in his mind where he sees himself looking normal, calm, and friendly. He's smiling as they're talking, and not only is there nothing weird about him, he looks like a nice guy. The visualization can boost the power of the new thought.

POWER THOUGHTS

So we can replace negative thoughts with more reasonable thoughts. Not with thoughts that are ridiculously positive or upbeat, but with reasonable, helpful thoughts. If we can replace negative thoughts with more helpful thoughts, can we also just add in new thoughts on their own? Thoughts that are helpful but don't necessarily replace anything? Yes! Absolutely!

Power thoughts, or coping thoughts, can be enormously helpful. You don't have to build these thoughts solely as a response to a negative, opposing thought; rather you can build these thoughts preventively. You can create a reserve of thoughts that empower you, and make you feel confident and strong. This reserve is something you can hold on to and look at both in times of comfort and times of distress. And the more you practice these power thoughts, the stronger the neural pathways and the more accessible the thoughts.

What's your favorite quote? I'm a huge fan of inspirational quotes, and I even had some put onto a keychain fob that I carry around with me. One of my favorite quotes is from a Clive James poem: "Remember this day, it's already melting." That's a quote I use when I want to savor an experience. It reminds me that our days are short and time is precious. Or when I want to keep going even though it's really hard and it would be easier to just quit, I'll repeat to myself (and this is a little embarrassing) "Just keep swimming." That quote is from Dory in *Finding Nemo*. Silly, but it works to motivate me. What are the quotes that motivate you, and when do you use them?

Once you have your quotes identified, and you know when you want to use them, choose your favorite. Write it down, make it look awesome, and carry it around with you—maybe as a note or a reminder in your phone, or on a sticky note you put on your bedroom mirror where you can see it in the mornings, or on a little ornament you can put on your keychain. Start reading your quote to yourself in different settings (you'll learn more about why this works so well in Chapter 7) and in different emotional states (you already know why this works), and make sure to repeat it to yourself multiple times throughout the day. You'll know the neural path is getting established when the quote comes to you unbidden when you need it. That is proof not only of the power of plasticity but also of the power of your effort.

PRIME YOUR BRAIN

As you now know, changing your thoughts actually creates change in your brain. When you change your thoughts, you build new neural pathways. The more you practice thinking these new thoughts, the stronger the new neural pathways and the less likely you are to retreat back to the old mal-adaptive ways of thinking. It's a process that takes time, and it works. But sometimes we need to change our thoughts quickly; it's worth sacrificing long-term change to feel better ASAP.

A study at Stanford by Dr. Gordon Bower actually showed how our thoughts can make us much more sad than we originally were. (Don't worry, the next study does the opposite.) He used hypnosis to do something called brain priming. Have you ever painted a room? Usually the first step is to put primer down on the wall. Primer blocks the old color so it doesn't show through, and it also makes it easier for the new color to stick to the wall. Brain priming is kind of similar; it gets rid of an old mood and sets the brain up to feel a certain way.

Using hypnosis, Dr. Bower was able to get the study participants feeling very sad, and then he started to notice where their thoughts went. Rainbows, ponies, and kittens? Nope. They thought about mistakes they had made and sad memories, and they focused more on negative words (Bower 1981) .

Brain priming can also work the other way, where positive moods can contribute to positive thoughts, and, in turn, get people to focus more on what is good and right about their life rather than what is wrong. Dr. Alice Isen and colleagues at Cornell University used brain priming to directly lift people's moods and indirectly increase their creativity. She showed one group of participants a really funny movie; the other group had no movie. All the participants were then tested on their creative thinking abilities. The people who had watched the funny movie were able to show a lot more creative thinking than the other folks (Isen, Daubman, and Nowicki 1987).

I used to practice brain priming once a week with my officemate. We both had very long days on Thursdays, and we were usually fried by the end of the workday. We knew these were our hardest days, and we set up a routine to stay late at work on those days. We would watch shows like *SNL*, *Veep,* and *Curb Your Enthusiasm*. We literally made plans just to laugh together as much as possible, and it was serious fun. Not only was there the pleasure of looking forward to the event, there was the actual laughter itself, the shared experience, and then the memories of laughing that we carried forward. Try this out (the second part where you feel better—not the first). What is the funniest show you have ever watched? Is it a YouTube video, some random meme from an app, a movie, or a TV show? Make a quick list of five things that you're confident will make you laugh.

Try scheduling a regular time to watch whatever you chose. Don't make it too long a time; thirty or forty-five minutes is plenty. If possible, include someone else. We know that the teen brain loves social connection, and adding another person (even virtually) will amplify the positivity of the experience. But no worries if no one can join you—do it on your own. Make sure to schedule the time so you can look forward to it. There is research showing that a big part of the awesomeness of vacations is the anticipation of the event. The same applies here. You get joy from anticipating, doing, and then remembering these experiences of doing something good for your brain and your mood.

BRAIN HACK: Laugh out loud.

Laughter boosts your mood, activates your immune system, and stimulates your organs. (Sounds gross, but it's actually a good thing.) Laughter has been shown to reduce stress responses and increase emotional flexibility. We all find different things funny, but find *your* humor and laugh much and often (Savage et al. 2017).

Thoughts matter. A random bizarre thought is no big deal, that's normal and it happens to everyone, but thinking the same negative things over and over is a problem. We end up inadvertently strengthening those thoughts (remember, what fires together, wires together). We don't mean to do this. No one wants to reinforce the negative, but we actually have to deliberately work at building the positive neural pathways. Luckily, this is possible. You can do it. So start catching and changing those thoughts, build up your power thoughts, prime your brain for happiness, and savor experiences.

When you learn to catch thoughts, you can start to change thoughts. You can also recognize your negative thoughts and learn more about what's bringing you down. Stress is one of the biggest feelings you have to manage in the teen years, and your thoughts can make that stress bigger or they can help you hack into the stress energy and use it to your advantage. Knowing how to work with your thoughts makes a big difference in how you manage your stress.

Read on to learn more. Using a mix of CBT and neuroscience, you're going to find out how to change your entire perspective on stress so you can move out of anxiety and fear and move into doing what you want to do.

CHAPTER 4

Stress: The Good and the Bad

The good news is that stress can be helpful. Really. Stress can motivate you to complete a project, meet a deadline, and run faster in your track meet. The bad news is that too much stress can be a problem. The teen brain is very vulnerable to stress. Stress can actually shrink some of the cells in the hippocampus and amygdala, causing memory loss and increased reactivity. The even worse news is that social stress (stress about friends and fitting in) is at its absolute highest levels during adolescence (Shellenbarger 2016). But there are ways to think about stress differently that can actually change how your brain and body react to it.

The experience of stress is temporary, and when you understand your stress response better, you can navigate it more effectively. You can even learn to use it to your advantage by thinking of stressful situations as challenges rather than stressors.

STRESS IN YOUR BRAIN AND BODY

In earlier chapters, we talked about the fight, flight, or freeze response. It's a real thing and important to understand, but it isn't the only stress response. We're going to start by looking at how the fight, flight, or freeze response works in your brain and body, and then look at how to move out of it and into other, more helpful stress responses.

The fight, flight, or freeze response occurs when your brain perceives a threat and activates your limbic system. We will be talking mostly about the amygdala, hippocampus, and hypothalamus, but your limbic system is made up of multiple parts: the amygdala, hippocampus, thalamus, hypothalamus, basal ganglia, and cingulate gyrus. It is the emotional center of your brain, responsible for communicating to your PFC and other parts of your brain.

When you have a thought that is fearful, tense, negative—or really any big emotional response—this thought sends a signal to the amygdala letting it know there is a threat. The amygdala responds by reaching out to your hypothalamus. The hypothalamus is the control center of the brain, and once it knows there's a problem, it activates the autonomic nervous system.

The autonomic nervous system controls involuntary actions like breathing, heart rate, and blood pressure. It turns on the sympathetic nervous system, which sends a message throughout the body to prepare for action. The hormones cortisol and adrenaline are released, and these chemicals let your body know it's time to get serious. Adrenaline allows you to experience your environment more clearly: your pupils dilate so more light comes in, your hearing gets more clear, and your mind takes in information even faster than it had been before. You are suddenly very aware and focused on your immediate environment. Your liver starts releasing fat and sugar into your blood to provide a ready source of fuel. You start breathing more deeply and taking in more oxygen so that your heart is beating fast, ready to move that sugar and fat to your muscles and your brain.

Essentially, you're prepared to face whatever is coming your way with strength and power.

Will, a fifteen-year-old, knows this fight, flight, or freeze reaction well. He's a seriously good kid, but you wouldn't know it if you saw him in the middle of responding to stress. Will's brain tends to go toward the fighting response when he is overwhelmed with emotion. He feels the blood racing through his body, his fists automatically clench, and he describes his whole body as feeling like it's tight and ready to go. Will doesn't like this response. It gets him into trouble, it makes kids steer clear from him, and it makes him look mean—which he isn't.

The limbic system may process emotions differently for some kids, and they may feel things much more intensely than others. And, since the teen brain is already so primed and reactive, adolescence can be even tougher for these kids. Will is a kid who has big emotional responses. He can't change his responses, but he can change how he thinks about them and what he does about them. As you probably noticed, I am repeating the CBT idea that feelings are changed by how we think and/or how we act (our behaviors).

Will is invested in changing his anger responses; he really wants to do this. He starts by collecting his automatic thoughts, and pretty quickly there is a clear pattern:

This isn't fair!

He can't do this to me!

He's trying to humiliate me!

Can you see a pattern emerging just from those three thoughts? In CBT, we think of anger arising when someone violates us in some way—our space, our rights, our beliefs, and so on. Will's automatic thoughts show that his limbic system reacts strongly to the idea that people are treating him badly or unfairly. He has a strong sense of justice and of right and wrong.

Once Will realizes that his anger gets quickly activated when he perceives himself being mistreated, he now has a powerful clue. If he can work to anticipate situations that will lead to this type of perception—a teacher who he knows is always hard on him, a kid who teases him, and so on, he can prepare for those situations. Instead of going into a situation with his vulnerability open and exposed, he can go in knowing that he is at risk of losing his cool. This knowledge affords him a couple of benefits:

He anticipates his response. You know how when you know the end of a scary movie, the movie is less scary? The same is true here. Will knows that he is likely to overreact, and knowing that means the response will have less power over him.

He can prepare for the attack. Again, if you know something is likely to happen, you can armor yourself appropriately. In this case, Will can practice his mantra, use coping thoughts, or just visualize himself staying calm and strong in the face of the onslaught. How Will thinks during these initial moments of stress can truly change his body's response. Yep, our thoughts can turn up or down the dial of our physical responses.

Fight, flight, or freeze made sense in the past, when our ancestors fought wild animals, lived in dangerous conditions, and were just trying to survive. Will isn't facing any of those things. He isn't fighting lions on the way to school or sleeping outdoors under trees or in caves. But his brain is reacting as if he were. His brain is treating minor situations like big, huge, dangerous events. But we know this, and knowledge is power (at least in this case). So Will can adapt his thoughts, adjust his behavior, and work preventively to manage the potential over-reaction.

BRAIN HACK: Get on top of your automatic stress response by learning to tighten and relax your muscles deliberately.

During times of stress, our brain asks our muscles to tighten up to prepare for something bad that might happen. The longer we stay tight, the more our brain thinks we need to be tight. It's a feedback loop. But you can hack out of this process through a practice of tightening and relaxing your muscles, going one body part at a time from your face on through your entire body. This is called progressive muscle relaxation. Try practicing once a day, every day, for the next week or so to see what happens to the stress you feel. The easiest time to start your practice is generally when you're going to bed at night. You're starting to relax, maybe some thoughts are creeping in, and your body is ready to let go of stress. This is your moment to help your body and brain reduce the stress. The loosening or relaxing of our muscles in this way can trick our brains into thinking the danger that can otherwise overwhelm us is past (McGonigal 2015).

THE NINETY-SECOND RULE

The initial stress response, when your hormones turn on and release into your bloodstream, is out of your control. But it is only out of your control for ninety seconds. Ninety seconds is how long it takes for the initial burst of chemicals that trigger your fight, flight, or freeze response to flush in and out of your bloodstream. A neuroscientist named Jill Bolte Taylor has found that there are two ways this response can go. You can feel the stress, the rush of chemicals, and continue to think and act in ways that incite your amygdala, thus causing this ninety-second response to go into repeat mode. Or you can change how you're thinking and actually change how your body responds. You can pull out of the ninety-second loop and move on (Taylor 2006).

The first step to using this ninety-second rule is to notice when you're having a stress response. This can be surprisingly difficult, and we each have different clues to alert ourselves to our responses. Will, as you know, has a stress response where his fists clench and his body tightens. His thoughts reflect his anger at the world and his situation. Lily, a seventeen-year-old, doesn't notice any physical changes, but she finds her thoughts shift quickly to the negative. She catches thoughts like *I can't do this. This is impossible; no one can do this. I can't believe how unfair this is.* These are not unusual responses to stress, and there is no right or wrong way to experience stress. Stress responses are as unique as the person having them.

What's your response to stress? Take some time to journal about it now, or after the next chance you have to observe how your brain and body react to the things that stress you out. Paying attention to your personal response lets you learn to recognize when you're moving into this state of arousal, and lets you practice strategies to stop the loop from repeating.

Once you're able to recognize the start of the ninety-second stress response, you can begin to change it. Here's how:

1. Recognize the feeling you're experiencing. An emotion is a neurological response to your perception of a situation. So, when you sense you're in the grip of a strong emotion, name what you're feeling and allow yourself to fully experience that emotion—even if that means feeling uncomfortable.

2. Ask yourself, *What is the stress telling me?* Identify the specific things that are causing you to feel stress.

3. Write down the stressors. Putting the words on paper moves them from abstract ideas in your head into concrete concepts on paper.

4. Change the thought or the behavior. Make the thought realistic and helpful, and look at what you can do to reduce the stress (maybe this means actually making a list, starting a project, or practicing self-care).

BRAIN HACK: Hug yourself.

A study found that when you cross your arms against your chest, essentially giving yourself a hug, pain is noticeably reduced and positive feelings are increased. During stressful moments a (private) self-hug can actually make you feel better (Gallace et al. 2011).

FEEL THE STRESS

A longitudinal study from the early 2000s changed the way scientists think about stress. In that study, researchers found that (in adults) self-reported high levels of stress increased the risk of death by 43 percent. Forty-three percent! *But,* and this is important, it increased the risk of death only in participants who believed that stress was harmful. Those who had stress but didn't believe stress was harmful were the lowest risk in the study (Keller et al. 2012).

There are a number of problems with viewing stress as unequivocally harmful. As you've learned, your body believes what you tell it, and if you tell your brain that stress is harmful, it gets to work pumping out chemicals to neutralize the "harmful" stress. This process, with all the hormones and chemicals being released, can make you feel more tired and less able to function. When our brain tries to help us by chemically dulling our stress, it takes a toll.

Additionally, if we view stress as unequivocally harmful, we will try to avoid it. And by we, I mean everyone, not just teens. It's human nature to avoid things that make us uncomfortable. But again, avoidance actually makes things worse. When we avoid stress, or when we avoid any negative feelings, they tend to hang around in our brains and our bodies looking for a way out. Ultimately, avoidance does not help since it tends to make what we avoid, whether that's uncomfortable feelings, anxiety-provoking situations, or stressors, that much harder to deal with.

In a study done at a hospital trauma center in Ohio, researchers looked at the cost of stress avoidance. The participants were people who had just come to the ER after a major traffic accident. They had their urine tested for stress hormones upon arrival at the hospital. As the research progressed, the scientists began to be able to predict which of the participants would develop post-traumatic stress disorder (PTSD) just from the cortisol present in their urine when they were admitted to the ER. In a surprising twist (at least in my opinion), the people who had the highest levels of cortisol at the time of the accident were the least likely to develop PTSD. Let me repeat that: the participants who were the most stressed at the time of admission were the least likely to get PTSD. The people who had the lower levels of stress hormones were far more likely to develop PTSD (McGonigal 2015).

How does this make sense? More stress means you do better? Actually, yes—if you learn to deal with stress well. The theory is that when you're able to truly feel stress, to experience its full impact without struggling with it or trying to suppress it, you're more able to move through the stress response and back to healthy functioning. The flip side is that avoiding the stress, or not actually experiencing stress, costs your brain and your body more. In other words, experiencing stress is rough in the short run, but it pays off long term.

What this means for you is that it's okay to feel uncomfortable and get through it. In fact, when we're able to notice our stress and move through it with awareness, we're better able to change how we perceive it.

USING YOUR STRESS

If you think about it, stress can sometimes feel good. You know that feeling when you're super motivated (finally!) to do the thing you've been putting off? That is what Stanford researcher Dr. Kelly McGonigal calls a "chemical cocktail of endorphins, adrenaline, testosterone, and dopamine." This "excite and delight" side of stress is the fun kind: riding a roller coaster, performing in a play on stage, racing for the ball in a playoff game (McGonigal 2015).

What's more, have you ever noticed that you can sometimes get more done when you feel stress or pressure to complete a task? A deadline, people counting on you, or being in a new situation can actually elicit stress, and, for most of us, that leads to our being fueled by our stress and actually becoming more motivated. It turns out that how we think about our stress, and how we use our stress, matters most.

In both these cases, we have the same symptoms but we change the meaning. A stronger physical stress response is actually good. When people with anxiety disorders have a stronger physical stress response, it actually changes the meaning and outcome of their anxiety. If they are able to label and understand the physical feeling of anxiety (remember name to tame?), they are less likely to get caught up in the swirling underlying thoughts. As you know from Chapter 3, our thoughts can drive and increase our anxiety. But when we feel our anxiety in our body, if we can notice it and label it, we do better. Participants had more confidence and better responses under pressure and scrutiny. Embracing anxiety, feeling it and relabeling it, leads to better outcomes (Kircanski, Lieberman, and Craske 2012).

The challenge response—when you perform well under pressure—is a type of stress response that actually makes you feel more self-confident, encourages action, and enables you to learn from experience. Your heart rate rises, and the hormones release, but instead of complete panic or fear, you feel a sense of excitement and focus. The difference between fight, flight, or freeze and the challenge response is literally a difference in chemicals. And we do have some influence over which chemicals our bodies and brains choose to release, if we can cultivate awareness of what we feel and think when stressors arise. When we believe that our stress is helping us, we have greater available resources and better heart function (Jamieson, Nock, and Mendes 2012.)

The hormone DHEA (dehydroepiandrosterone) is a key factor in how you react to stress. When there are higher levels of DHEA in your stress response, you handle the stress better and you learn from the experience. It's like your brain is saying "this is hard, but you can do it" (in contrast to the fight, flight, or freeze response where your brain is just saying "Arrghhhh!").

BRAIN HACK: Choose excitement!

The next time you're feeling major stress about an upcoming presentation or event, challenge yourself to see if you can be excited about whatever it is you're working on, not just nervous or afraid. Practice this by literally saying *I am excited!* in your head or aloud. The truth is, stress, anxiety, and excitement are different forms of the same fundamental phenomenon; they're all forms of arousal. More importantly, though, research has shown that seeing the stress you feel as a kind of excitement increases your ability to perform at a higher level (Crum et al. 2013).

Another major stress response, again defined by Dr. McGonigal, is the tend-and-befriend response. This response involves seeking out others to assist you with whatever is causing your stress. This kind of connection with others actually produces oxytocin, which causes you to feel a little more courageous and a lot closer to the people around you. Dr. McGonigal hypothesizes that this response served an evolutionary process in encouraging our ancestors to seek out others and thereby build their community and safety network. In today's world, it can help you build the kinds of friendships and connections that can help you deal with things that would otherwise be very challenging (McGonigal 2015).

STRESS AND MEANING ARE RELATED

Imagine it's mid-January. It's getting dark in the afternoons, the weather is colder, you have a million things due for school, there's a test almost every day, and you start dreaming about summer vacation. You imagine all the free time you will have to just do nothing. Sound good? Usually this type of fantasy feels great at the time, but when summer rolls around and you truly are doing nothing, it gets a little old.

Humans need meaning in their lives, and this is especially true for you as a teen. At this point in your life, you're likely seeking meaning in a deep and passionate way. As much as you might dream about doing nothing, it often isn't quite as good as you think it will be. In fact, many teens report feeling bored and listless over the summer when they are just lying around the house.

It probably doesn't surprise you to know that stress and meaning are linked. People who experience less stress often feel their lives are less meaningful. In fact, a Stanford and University of Florida study found that people who had experienced the most stress in their past were more likely to consider their current lives meaningful. (McGonigal 2015). The key is to know how to deal with stress, just as you've been learning to do—and to find the things that will be rewarding even if they involve some hard work and some pain.

STRESS AND EXCITEMENT ARE RELATED

Stress and excitement are related. So is risk. Some of the hormones released with stress include cortisol, adrenaline, and norepinephrine. The same hormones can be released when we're very excited. When you get super excited or super stressed, you're in what psychologists refer to as a state of arousal; your brain is activated and releasing hormones to support your mood. When we're in a situation where we face risk, the hormones released can mimic those of excitement. In fact, for many teens, the state of risk feels like stress and excitement.

There are some obvious problems with risk feeling positive to teens. Your brain is just begging for excitement, and risk often feels very appealing during adolescence. Using your new knowledge about stress, we're going to move next into one of the most challenging parts of being a teen: the drive for risk and reward. This is what makes being a teenager one of the most dangerous times in your life, and the more you know about your brain and how to manage it, the better it is for you and those around you.

CHAPTER 5

Risk, Excitement, and Drama: Your Brain Wants It All

I can still clearly remember my tenth-grade driver's ed class. Mr. Sutton played movies for us with titles like *Highway of Death* and *The Road to Your Grave.* (Okay, I made the second one up, but it's not far off.) The images of gory accident scenes were meant to scare us into understanding the risks of speeding or driving while distracted. And these images may not have changed my driving habits (more on that later), but they certainly stuck with me.

The reason for the graphic images in driver's ed classes is because adults hope to scare teens into acting with caution. Adolescence is the highest risk time for death by accident, homicide, or suicide (Steinberg 2014). And car accidents in particular are by far the biggest cause of death in adolescence, accounting for well over two thousand deaths in 2018 alone. This breaks down to more than seven teens per day dying in car crashes and hundreds of teens being injured on a daily basis (CDC 2020).

But the issue isn't that teens don't understand the risks of, say, driving super fast; you actually do know that certain behaviors are more dangerous. Your brain is excellent at reasoning, and by your late teens your memory and intelligence will be equal to your adult level (Steinberg 2014). The problem is that even though you know this, you still are drawn to the risky behaviors. Your brain is seeking positive and new experiences and feelings.

We can blame dopamine for this pleasure-seeking drive in adolescence. Our PFC and limbic system are always in communication, however imperfect (because they are not fully wired yet). The limbic system creates the emotional response to a situation, and the PFC helps decide how to respond to that situation. The PFC keeps us from chasing after every butterfly flitting by (or whatever it may be that tempts us), but the limbic system can up the ante by increasing the strength of the emotions we experience. The stronger the emotion, the more likely we are to follow it. And some people just have limbic systems that seem to feel things more. As a teen, your limbic system feels things intensely. It is constantly challenging your PFC by insisting that big feelings be given a level of importance. So what's the PFC to do?

Let's dig into this relationship between emotion and reaction or risk and reward in the teen brain so we can figure out why risky things feel so tempting to you right now—and how you can navigate this so you can learn to try out new things, which is part of being a teen, without taking on dangerous risk.

REWARD FEELS AMAZING TO TEENS

Why is adolescence such a dangerous time? Social scientists believe that teens' brains focus on pleasure and reward more than risk for an evolutionary reason. Because this age has typically meant leaving home, increasing independence, and exploring new situations and environments, teens actually need to feel a little braver. To put it another way, the adolescent brain seeks intense, new, and exciting experiences. And a big part of this is attributed to changes in the *ventral striatum.*

The ventral striatum is located deep in the middle of your brain, and it plays a significant role in reward and motivation. The ventral striatum goes through significant changes in adolescence. These changes make your brain much more sensitive to rewards than at any other time in your life. Your brain wants to feel good, it wants new experiences, and it is always looking for rewards. Adolescent rats are twice as likely to use drugs as adult rats. Obviously you're not a rat, but you're much more likely to seek new experiences that feel good (Galván 2013). These experiences can range from trying things that taste good, to seeking thrills, to trying to make a quick buck. Unfortunately, you may not be aware enough of the consequences of the things you try.

Driving is a great example. In one study, teens who ran a yellow light had a boost of blood flow to the ventral striatum when they zipped through. But, if their mom was in the car with them when they ran the light, their brain did not reward them for risky behavior. In fact, if their mom was in the car with them, they had much more activity in the PFC (thinking part) and less blood flow to the ventral striatum (Telzer, Ichien, and Qu 2015).

This study shows that adolescence brings both an increase in risk-taking and a decrease in impulse control. Ouch! That is not a good combination. Having your mom or a grownup who matters with you can help you rein in that tendency, kind of acting like your PFC for you, but how do you do this for yourself? If you don't, you could easily hurt yourself or someone else. Remember, your limbic system is jumping around yelling "Big emotions!" and your poor PFC is struggling to figure out which ones to regulate and which ones to let go.

Another study looking at adolescent risk-taking involved a simulated gambling activity. (Gambling studies with teens seems to be a common interest for researchers.) In the study, teen responses were compared to adult responses. And, unsurprisingly, not only did adolescents take the most risks (right around age fifteen was the highest risk point), they also felt the most regret or relief after the task. Emotions were higher for seeking rewards (bet more!) as well. An amplifier plugged into a guitar makes the sound much louder, and same idea holds for your teen brain. Only it isn't your guitar that's getting amplified; it's your emotions. This, coupled with an unparalleled drive to feel good and have new experiences, makes for some challenges (Blakemore 2018).

Helen, seventeen, told me a story about going for a drive for friends. They were having a great time; the music was on and the windows were down, and she felt fantastic. She was driving and didn't realize how fast she was going. She was so into the experience and feeling "so alive." But when she saw a police car she felt an immediate knot in her stomach, her foot leapt off the gas pedal, and she put both hands on the steering wheel. The story is anticlimactic because she didn't get pulled over, but it took that external cue to pull her out of her thoughtless but joy-filled state. And, once she saw the police car, she was out of the "trance" and back in reality.

Up until the point when Helen saw the police car, her limbic system was in charge. She was just enjoying the moment, and she wasn't thinking about the danger of speed or the risk of a ticket. The sight of the police officer switched her limbic system from pleasure to fear. The good news is that this experience scared her (Good work, limbic system! This was an appropriate time to feel fear), but the bad news is that her PFC had not taken over. She wasn't thinking through situations—she was just following her feelings.

BRAIN HACK: Use visualization to activate your PFC and get control.

If you catch yourself in a period of time where things feel a little too good and a little out of control, visualize your mom, your teacher, a police officer, or any authority figure, and see how you respond. If you get that sick feeling in your stomach, it means your ventral striatum is taking over and you need to get your PFC back in action.

Luckily, Helen knows the basics of CBT, and she realized that if she could start catching, checking, and changing her automatic thoughts, she might be able to get more information about what was going on for her personally. She also might be able to use them to get her PFC working a little more. So Helen thinks back to that night and that drive. She's not 100 percent certain of the exact thoughts, but she thinks they were some-thing like: *This is amazing. I want to make this night awesome for everyone. I want them to want to hang out with me all the time.*

There are some good parts to those thoughts, but can you also see where the challenge is? If Helen is feeling so good, if she attributes this "so good" feeling to driving fast and reckless, does that mean she needs to do that whenever she wants to feel good? It sounds almost silly, but actually, yes. Your teen brain really wants dopamine. If it feels like fast driving is the way to get it, then it will push you to do it again and again. When you hear about people "chasing the high," it means chasing the good feeling. At no other time in your life will your brain be so vulnerable to starting habits that involve chasing that high.

You probably noticed the other automatic thought that Helen remembered: *I want them to want to hang out with me all the time.* If I were with Helen, I would want to hear a lot more about that thought. I can't be sure, but it kind of implies that she doesn't think they do want to hang out with her all the time. When you have this happen, when you catch an automatic thought that seems to have a bigger or deeper meaning, it's time to explore it. Write it down (the act of writing engages more of your brain, from your lovely PFC to the parts that control hand movements, the speech center, and more) and ask yourself: *What would it mean if* [insert the fear the thought seems to imply and what it would mean about you]. So Helen's thought *I want them to want to hang out with me all the time* might be phrased like this: *What would it mean if they didn't really want to hang out with me? What would that say about me?*

As Helen thought this over, she started to realize that she does worry about her friends really wanting to be with her. Sometimes she feels like she's on the edge of the group, not fully in the group. And she worries that they really don't want to hang out with her because she's kind of introverted and boring. Let me be clear—Helen is introverted, but she is *not* boring. Nonetheless she feels boring, and she worries that kids think that about her.

This is great insight on Helen's part, and something we want to explore further, but it also lets us know a couple of Helen's vulnerabilities. She is worried about being boring, which she might try to compensate for by doing things like driving too fast. And she is not sure she fits in with her group. Which means she's more vulnerable to doing things that she thinks will make kids like her more. This is not bad. Helen is not unique or unusual. She struggles with things most teens struggle with, and it's totally okay and normal. What's different about Helen is that she is doing the work to figure out where she is vulnerable so that she can shore up that area and not give in to these risky impulses without thought.

Helen's story illustrates the complicated nature of the brain and risk as a teen. You already know about peer influence, and her story gives a glimpse as to how that happens. Peers actually do make a big difference in how you will act in certain situations, and the next section looks further at this.

RISK ALONE VS. RISK WITH FRIENDS

You are significantly more likely to do something dumb if you are with friends. I once asked a fifteen-year-old boy I work with if he would ever jump into the Potomac River (a big, dirty river near where I live in Washington, DC). He laughed and said, "No way!" (A favorite science experiment for kids in the DC area is to show the levels of *E.coli* in the water—it's never a low number.) I then named five of his friends. These were kids he talked about a lot, and the kids he tended to hang out with outside of school. "So if A, B, C, D, and E all jumped into the river in some silly prank, you wouldn't do it?" He laughed again. "Okay, I might if we were doing it together." If he had really thought that through, he probably would have caught himself (we all resist the idea that we're influenced by peers), but he answered quickly and honestly. We all are more likely to do something if others are doing it, but you, as a teen, are much, much more likely to do it. And without foreknowledge, you won't even realize that you're doing it. It just seems so normal and natural.

Have you had this experience—being tempted to do something because it was new or fun, even if you knew it might not be the best or safest thing to do in that moment? We all have this experience sometimes.

The key, as always, is to slow down long enough to really understand what you're thinking and feeling in such moments, and then to realistically observe the situation you're in, in order to make a conscious choice about how you want to act, beyond what your ventral striatum is driving you to do. Obviously I'm making this sound much easier than it really is, but I think you get the idea, and I'm sure you've done it before. Think back to a time when you did slow down your reaction (and were so glad that you did!)

BRAIN HACK: Fully engage your PFC!

By planning for risks you choose to use your PFC rather than just responding to the emotion of the limbic system. Knowing ahead of time what your risks are makes a difference. If you know that you're tempted to drive fast and weave between cars even though there are a lot of other people on the road, or that you want to go with a cool new friend to a huge party even though you don't really know anyone there, you can consciously change how you think about the situation. And you get to *choose* not to give in to the urge rather than unintentionally following the path your brain leads you down. Ultimately, this is your decision. But, as with all decisions, it's best to make the choice fully aware of all the factors—and sometimes, with our automatic behaviors, we're less aware of all the factors at play than we could be.

And there are other ways to hack your overactive reward system. Focusing on what you value in life can help you decide if a particular behavior is one you actually want to do—if a particular risk is one you want to take. You have your own moral compass, and that still works, no matter how active your ventral striatum may be. It takes a conscious effort to check in with yourself about what you believe and what you think is right, but it's an effort worth making.

Be aware, the teen brain can be manipulated, and people always seem ready to try. It is no accident that cigarette and vape manufacturers target teens; the teen brain is a vulnerable target in the world of advertising. If you can stay true to your core values despite the pressure, you will tend to feel happier. For example, teens were less likely to smoke if they were told that secondhand smoke harms those around them; trying to scare them with pictures of gross lungs was ineffective. And, in the same vein, teens were more likely to eat healthy if they were told that big food companies were trying to manipulate them into eating junk food through ads and other media. In other words, if you can connect the behavior you want (to exercise or eat healthy) to some broader social value you hold, like your love for your family or your desire to make your decisions for yourself rather than for a company who wants you to behave a certain way, you will be more successful (Blakemore 2018).

Another strategy for reducing your likelihood of risk is to challenge yourself not to do what you're tempted to do. That is, to use your self-talk. I have the hardest time talking teens into using this most helpful strategy, and the main reason is because it's "too basic." But sometimes there's a reason why basic things work. Self-talk is one of the most effective strategies for changing your thoughts and your behavior. Helen from the previous section might use self-talk like this: "Helen, you want these kids to like you. You want to prove you're not boring, but you can do this in other, safer ways. Remember that time you guys all walked around downtown and just laughed and told stories? That was just as fun as the time you guys spent

driving. Helen, they do like you (they hang out with you all the time), and you don't have to keep proving it."

That's one example, but now let's look further at self-talk. It's one of my personal favorite strategies ("Elisa, keep writing. Do not pick up your phone. Stay focused and write. You can do hard things.") and my hope is to convince you to give it a try. The next section looks at self-talk and how it works.

TALKING TO YOURSELF

Self-talk is quite literally talking to yourself. No matter whether or not we admit it, we all talk to ourselves. But my experience is that teens often talk to themselves in a very negative way. Remember the core beliefs we talked about in Chapter 1? The beliefs we hold about ourselves, others, and the world? Often these beliefs show up in the way we talk to ourselves. If you have the belief that something is wrong with you, that you are defective in some way, then you might have thoughts like *I can never do anything right* or *I always screw up*.

Here's the weird part. Sometimes we aren't even aware that we're having these automatic thoughts. Automatic thoughts are just below the surface of our awareness, and they reflect something about ourselves. When Helen dug into her automatic thoughts, she realized she was taking risks because of deeper fears about fitting in or being thought of as boring.

If you start to notice your automatic thoughts, you will probably notice that they are not the most positive. It's surprisingly tricky to notice your thoughts, and I often ask teens to think back on an event and guess what their thoughts might have been. Ideally, you catch automatic thoughts in the moment, but looking back works if you're having a hard time coming up with any.

We want to know the automatic thoughts that come up when you're struggling with something, embarrassed, or having some negative emotion. Notice what is going through your mind—write it down or record it. Once you get used to catching these thoughts, you can start to find patterns. Maybe you always tell yourself that you're "weird," "awkward," or "embarrassing." Or maybe you start to realize that you actually call yourself names and criticize yourself. One kid I know routinely tells herself she's an "idiot," "clueless," or just "not smart at all." She would never talk to another person that way, but she regularly speaks to herself like that.

Self-talk is a powerful tool that can be used to engage the PFC, while making some of these age-appropriate brain tendencies less mindless. In other words, your brain is going to do what it wants to do right now, but you actually can change both your brain itself and your behaviors by using self-talk. When you deliberately tell yourself what you want yourself to do (I know, it sounds nuts) you pull in the PFC and move out of the limbic system's overreactions.

What about you? What risky things do you sometimes feel tempted to do? And what could you say to yourself in such moments to slow down and pull yourself out of amygdala-driven behavior and back into your PFC? Try to avoid judging yourself for wanting to do risky things. As you've seen, it's normal to want to do them at your age. What's amazing is that you're actually working on ways to avoid giving in to those impulses.

Take a minute here to write down or think through things you could say to yourself if you start to take risks that don't fit with your beliefs and values. Self-talk works best when you're kind, compassionate, and instructive, so take it easy on yourself as you go through this. If you get stuck, think about how you would talk to a friend who was in the same situation. This is a good rule of thumb if you're someone who tends to talk negatively to yourself. Asking yourself *How would I say this to* _____ can help you notice the negativity and switch it up to more productive and effective self-talk.

I witnessed self-talk in action when I was teaching my son to drive. Unlike his big sister, who just took off when she learned, he started talking out loud to himself. He repeated instructions—"Turn on the clicker here, good, you've got this"— and he also praised himself. I'm not sure he was even aware that he was speaking out loud until I noticed it and complimented him on it. Of course, that was a rookie mistake on my part, and he completely stopped talking aloud after my comment, but my hope is that he continued talking about it in his head.

There's good research showing that self-talk helps you control your emotions, your thoughts, and your behaviors—but you have to do it the right way. Researchers at Michigan State University actually studied the way it works best. Referring to yourself by your name (rather than using "I") activates your medial prefrontal cortex (remember, the PFC is the thinking part of the brain), allowing you more control.

These researchers were interested in how other people speak to each other, and they noted that when we talk to others we invariably use their names to attract their attention. They theorized the same would be true when talking to ourselves, and the research was able to show that a third-person approach was more effective than generic self-talk. When we use self-talk effectively, we lower our heart rate, stress response, and become more in control of our emotions. We activate the PFC and pull ourselves out of the amygdala's path (Kross et al. 2014).

Self-talk is so important because it keeps your thinking brain on, reducing risk in the process. As you may have noticed, we're constantly looking for ways to keep your very awesome PFC engaged and alert. Positive and instructive self-talk is a fairly easy and straightforward way for you to keep yourself in the moment and aware of the risk and the reward. Which is good, because as a teen you're going to face risks, and your dopamine is going to want you to say "Yes!" to risks that may cause harm.

DRINKING, DRUGS, AND RISK

You are much more likely to drink too much and use drugs in your teenage years than at other times in your life. The rush of excitement (dopamine!) and peer approval (dopamine!) that is often associated with drinking, smoking, and other drugs is a hard one to ignore. It's kind of a perfect storm at this age. Your brain craves the new, the novel, it is pushing you to fit in with peers, and it is ready and willing to amplify any good feeling that comes your way.

Your limbic system is primed to overreact to emotions, your dopamine receptors are primed and sensitive, and your ventral striatum is hoping for new experiences and big feelings. All this can work together to get you to do things you wouldn't have done a few years ago and won't do a few years from now. There are the obvious concerns like legality and the dangers of driving while intoxicated, and there are the less obvious concerns about the actual effect on your brain. And research is showing that it actually does matter if you drink or do drugs in adolescence. In fact, one of the most striking things I learned when writing this book was the permanent damage that drinking and drugs can do to the developing adolescent brain. So many members of my generation—Gen X, *not* boomer—didn't know the risks and others ignored them, and I wonder if anything would be different if we had understood.

Your brain is more vulnerable because of all the change and growth that is occurring right now. Picture a new branch on a tree. It's thinner and easier to snap off than the solid growth of a limb. You can scar the bark with just a little scratch. It's the same with the new changes in your brain; they aren't established yet, and your brain is less protected from potential harm.

In the first chapter, I wrote about how you can change your IQ in your teen years. I cited a statistic from research that showed that about 30 percent of kids raised their IQ in adolescence, 30 percent stayed the same, and 30 percent lowered their IQ. It turns out that drinking and drugs can play a role in decreasing your IQ. And not just because you're more likely to be in an accident; they can decrease it by literally killing off parts of your brain. I'm not saying this as an adult who wants to shake a finger in your face and scare you; I'm saying this because research has shown it to be true. And I know that shaking a finger at you wouldn't do anything anyway. You have to understand and have motivation to protect your intelligence and your brain.

When you use drugs and alcohol as a teen, the gray matter that has been building up starts rapidly decreasing, and the white matter becomes thinner and less effective. Remember, gray matter is the building blocks of the brain—where the information is stored. White matter is how your brain communicates—the connections that zip back and forth between areas like the PFC and the limbic system. As a teen, you already have less white matter, making your brain more reactive, and substances can take away even more. Research is also finding negative effects on your memory,

Risk, Excitement, and Drama: Your Brain Wants It All

your attention span, and self-control. And it looks like some of these negative effects can be lasting (Lees et al. 2020).

A VULNERABLE BRAIN

It's easy to think *Kids have been doing this stuff forever, and most kids do just fine.* But as an adolescent therapist and the mom of three teenagers myself, I am surprised by the danger of even small amounts of drinking and drug use. This is truly new and terrifying research. It's also true that the risk of dying from an accident in adolescence is two to three hundred times more likely than it is when you're a child or an adult (Steinberg 2014). And, even if people in my generation did this and survived to tell, I find myself wondering if IQs were reduced during that time.

Your brain is seriously vulnerable to the effects of drinking and drugs right at the time that it is most invested in seeking rewards, like the pleasure of a new, cool experience or the respect and approval of your friends. This seems unfair and illogical, but it is what it is. Recent reports show that 40 percent of American high-school students drink every month and up to one-fifth of those teens binge drink each month. Adolescents still get in cars with teens who have been drinking and let them drive. Increasing numbers, some around 25 percent and some higher, report smoking marijuana at least monthly, 20 percent still smoke cigarettes, and around 35 percent vape regularly (Steinberg 2014).

What's your experience? Have you been around kids who drink and use drugs? Have you felt pressure to use when you weren't sure you wanted to? Used because you wanted to? This is a great moment to think about your relationship to drinking and drugs. If you do use, are you more likely to use in certain situations or with certain friends? Do you ever worry about how much you use? If you don't use, why not? What keeps you grounded so you don't feel the need? Is that something you can put into words and hang on to?

Adolescents understand risk. If you ask "How risky is having unprotected sex?" they will universally say that it's risky. But, if you ask "How would you compare the benefits of unprotected sex with the risks?" you will get different answers based on the age of the kid. Dr. Steinberg found that teens aged fourteen to seventeen are much more likely to respond that the benefits of unprotected sex outweigh the risks (Steinberg 2013). In other words, having unprotected sex is so pleasurable to the adolescent brain that even though they fully understand the risks (disease, infection, pregnancy), they may still choose the risky behavior.

The key to hack your brain's attraction to reward is, again, to know your values and what you really want—and to be aware of your thoughts in moments of temptation, and the thinking traps you might be falling into. The tools you've learned in this book will be helpful to you in doing this!

Despite understanding risk, adolescents really, really like rewards. Given a choice between a guaranteed five-dollar reward or a 50 percent chance to win ten dollars and 50 percent chance to come away with nothing, most adolescents will take the gamble. Adults will almost always choose the sure thing (Reyna et al. 2011). Do you see the problem here? Even though you intellectually get the cost of a behavior, you're more likely to take a dumb risk because you want the good feelings.

You, as an adolescent, feel rejection by peers deeply. In fact, there is no other time in your life when you will feel rejection as strongly as you do right now. This part of your brain, the part that manages this distress, is still developing, and it causes you to be particularly sensitive to peer rejection or exclusion (Blakemore and Mills 2014). This actually leads to more risk-taking behaviors. Because you have a strong incentive not to feel so bad, you're more likely to do risky things in order to get your peers' approval. Combine this with a ventral striatum that is actively seeking reward, and it's a tough combination to manage.

The next chapter will go into the friendship and peer factors that influence your brain. It will break down the responses you're most likely to have when you interact with your peers and what motivates those, and you'll learn how you can build the friendships and connections to others you need to handle your stress, feel good, and do whatever it is you want to do with your amazing teen brain.

CHAPTER 6

Peers: They Matter a Lot

Friendships in adolescence are different. When you were younger, who your friends were probably had a lot to do with where they lived, if your parents knew each other, or what activities you did together. As a teen, it's not as easy, in ways that are both good and bad. You may have more choice in whom you hang out with—and that might make the task of finding the people you really fit with and feel good around harder, not easier. A lot of kids miss the simplicity and security of their old friendships, but they also recognize that their new friendships are deeper. In fact, one of the things most teens want from a friend is the ability to share secrets, and to trust completely (Way 2013).

Of course, relationships that are this deep and intense can also affect you very deeply and intensely. In one study, kids ages ten to twelve said that friends were important, but that their self-worth wasn't affected by what their friends thought. Fast-forward and ask the same question of a group of thirteen-to-sixteen-year-olds, and it's a very different response. The teenagers reported feeling more personal success and self-worth when they were accepted by their peers. They also reported a greater sense of failure and low self-worth when they were rejected (Blakemore 2018). It makes sense: your brain is growing in new ways; your life is expanding in new ways;

you're trying new things and trying to figure out where you fit in, where your niche is.

Research has shown again and again that for young people, having a *reciprocated* friend—meaning you both like each other—protects you from some of the negative effects of stress or bullying. This is one of those findings that makes sense. If you have a close friend, you have emotional support, you have empathy, and you have some protection from things that often feel dangerous, like the judgments of others.

Struggling to find a group or just not fitting in with your current group feels absolutely terrible. As a teen, you actually feel loneliness and rejection much more strongly than you will at any other age in your life. And your brain wants you to be in a group because "groups" mean "safety." If you're in a group, you have people you can count on, people you can care for just as they care for you—which was important for survival in the past and is important for connection in the present.

Your brain is so invested in your finding a group that it makes you feel acutely terrible if you're alone, and it may push you to accept friendship even from people who may not have your best interests at heart. This isn't very helpful or motivating, of course. You don't usually want to talk to people when you feel miserable, and no one likes to think that their friends may not actually be their friends. And your brain may also give you a push toward kids you do like. This is a time to think about your friendships, the kids who support you and who you support back. Friendships are one of the few things that show up consistently on measures of happiness. Friends matter. But your brain has a secondary agenda here, and with this knowledge you need to make sure you're seeking friends who nourish and encourage you, rather than kids who bring you down.

Having this information about how your brain prioritizes friendships right now lets you work on prioritizing the type of friendships you want. You will feel a pull for friends, any friends, at this time in your life (it's those thoughts again), but you get to choose positive relationships. You can choose friendships that aren't about status as much as they're about feeling safe and able to grow and change. And, if you're like many teens, you may realize as you read this chapter that you've gotten stuck in some negative or even harmful relationships. Maybe you hang out with people who make you feel bad or even bully you, just because you want to have someone to hang out with. Now you know that your brain is pushing you toward relationships at any cost, and you can make deliberate and conscious choices about what you really want.

WHY PEERS MATTER

Imagine this: You are alone on a vast, open field with nothing other than dry grass in sight. It's hot, really hot. You don't see shelter anywhere, and you hear noises in the distance that send chills down your spine. Night is coming, and you're completely alone. You are not sure where to go or what to do, but you know you need protection.

This situation isn't a likely one for most modern teens, but go back a hundred thousand years, and it could have been a possibility. At that time, human beings were still in the midst of their evolutionary journey, living in small groups out in the wild, and safety was a big deal. Being alone was not a good option, and this is when your brain began the process of pushing you toward connection with others. Connection with others meant safety.

Fast-forward to this century, and meet Jackie. She's new at her high school, and she doesn't know a single person. She isn't alone on a vast savannah, but her amygdala still feels some of the same threat and anxiety. And she isn't facing deadly hyenas, but without a group, she feels very much alone against what she does face: her peers—other kids who might judge her or welcome her; she's not sure which.

FRIEND? OR NOT?

What are the qualities of a good friendship in the teen years? Some of the most desirable skills of friendship include the ability to take another's perspective, a sense of humor, impulse control (sounds weird, but if you think about it, it makes sense), and empathy (Allen et al. 2012). And the most protective factors good friendship can give you include a sense of security, someone to talk to, someone to learn from, and someone to help you solve problems.

Do you have good, strong, reciprocal friendships in your life right now? Take some time to think or maybe even journal about the ways in which your friendships are strong. You can also think about ways you can be a better friend to the people you're friends with, so that they can enjoy more of those protective factors of friendship from your company, and so you can keep your friendships strong for years to come.

Here's another thing: friendships in adolescence are fluid. That means they can change. Hopefully you have good friends in your life: people you can be yourself around, and who give you as much as you give them. Everyone deserves those. But if you're alone right now, that doesn't mean you'll be alone forever. In fact, you can make changes right now. Often, it starts with finding your niche.

FINDING A PLACE

Niche groups—groups of people who share common qualities, like similar interests—start forming in midadolescence, and knowing and owning your strengths helps you figure out which group you choose to be in. Did you notice that word "choose"? That's important because knowing about the way groups form in adolescence means you get to have more control and more choice in how you proceed.

Let's do a little self-research. Step one is to identify your strengths. List them all on a piece of paper—even if you don't think they matter. Collect everything you do and can do well and write these things down. Once you've done this, go through and circle your favorite strengths. For example, you might be a great piano player, but you just don't care that much about piano, so you decide not to circle it. You do, however, feel really good about your ability to get along with most people. (This is a real strength and it counts!) So you circle it.

Once you've identified your favorite strengths, start brainstorming how to connect with kids with similar interests. If you circled soccer, but you're not up to the school team, is there a local rec league you can join? If you circled art, but your schedule doesn't leave room for an art elective, take a look at your school's club list and find one that relates to art. If you don't think your high school has a club that meets your needs, you can actually start one of your own. Most high schools encourage students to start their own groups. (And, as a bonus, it looks good for college applications, if that's something you're thinking about.) Whatever you try, know that this is where you get to take back the reins and start creating or finding your niche group.

Ultimately, unconsciously going along with the status quo—with what other people think is popular—is understandable and easy to do. Status *is* a thing—we all instinctively look at others to see how "cool" they are. We measure how cool a person is using standards that are sometimes pretty shallow—like the way someone is groomed (that's a real thing!), how attractive we think they are, and whether they own cool things. And we all sometimes try to change our behavior in ways that will make others see us as cool people. This isn't to say you should start posing for all your selfies in sexualized postures with lots of luxury goods if you want to be seen as cool! But it does give you an awareness of your and everyone's tendency to unconsciously view certain things as higher status. Finally, everyone wants others to recognize them as valuable and accepted. These tendencies are all part of the way we've evolved as human beings. But, now that you know how it all works, you don't have to let yourself get quite as swept up in the flow. You can find the acceptance we all need without compromising your values or doing things that don't feel genuinely you. Again, the key is to know and own who you are.

YOU GOT THIS

Figuring out who you are and owning it, as is often noted, is easier said than done. It's a process, and it takes time to figure out, but you can begin to be the kind of person you want to be. Go through your social media posts and find the ones that you like best. If you don't post, find the images and quotes online that speak to you the most.

Once you've got a good group of images and quotes, take a look and see what they have in common. Did you choose images that all feature people? If so, what do they look like? What similarities and differences did you notice? Are there images that give you positive feelings? Are there traits you see in these pictures that you want to make your own? Take some notes and figure out what you're drawn to.

Now, are any of your choices quotes? Go through and carefully reread them. Which truly speak to you? Write those down in a separate place to use for inspiration, solace, or calm. Try to write them in a way that reflects their meaning to you. You can do this using words, images, or fonts. This might be a poster that you handwrite and illustrate; it might be images, words, and sentences cut out from a magazine; or it might be something completely unique that shows the meaning you find from the images and words.

What did this exercise tell you about what you value? Are you pursuing these values right now in the groups you're in? Are there new connections you could make that could help you get more of what you value in life?

When she did this exercise, Jackie found that she chose pictures of girls who were laughing or smiling. The kids looked happy and goofy in the pictures; no one was trying that hard to look cool. And as she looked closer, she realized that a lot of the pictures she liked had been taken outside. At her old school, Jackie had been part of the hiking club. As she looked through all her favorite pictures, she realized how much she missed hiking with friends. She decided to look into joining or starting a hiking club at her new school, so she could find new good friends. Jackie had been trying to figure out how to fit in without thinking about who she was and what she really loved.

Of course, anytime you try to make new friends or expand your social circle in some way, there's a risk: you might be rejected. Often, that fear of being rejected keeps us from being brave enough to reach out to new people, which is understandable when you look at the science behind it. In CBT we talk about the risk/reward ratio. Anytime we try something new, there is risk. But what is the potential reward? In this case, the potential reward is real connections and relationships. Not every attempt to connect will be successful, but is it worth the risk of rejection to try? I think so, but keep reading to understand why your brain makes this risk seem worse than it is. If you know your brain is exaggerating the facts, then my hope is that you keep pushing through to find what's really true.

CHAPTER 7

"School Is Your Job Right Now"

How many times have you heard that line? It's kind of weird, because the way your school success is measured doesn't really relate to how well you will do in college, or at a job. For example, for 88.5 percent of kids, SAT scores are not predictive of college success; and there's no correlation between GPA and future job success (Achor 2010). And yet there is a very large correlation between GPA, SAT scores, and college acceptance. This doesn't make sense, but it's all too real. Lucky for you, there are ways to learn better and more efficiently so that if you have to play this game, at least you're on a level field. It's also worth understanding how you learn, so you can keep learning and growing throughout your life.

The good news: Remember the ventral striatum? The part of your brain that is supersensitive to rewards in the teen years? The ventral striatum considers getting answers correct rewarding. This means that you can use your brain to motivate you. The more answers you get right, the more the striatum gets activated. Once it's activated, dopamine is released, you feel good, and you want to get even more right.

Your brain can learn more effectively and more efficiently. You just need to learn some tools and techniques to hack into your brain's powers. You will also need to resist the urge to repeat old ways of studying that are not effective. This is probably the hardest part; for whatever reason, we humans love to do the same thing over and over—even when it isn't really working. So let's take a look at how you can learn better.

MANY ROADS, ONE DESTINATION

I think that's an old proverb, but it works really well here as an analogy. If you were to try to get to point A, or a place we will call Knowledge, you can always take the same road to get there. You could put on the navigation software and have an electronic voice call out directions to you as you drove along. You would most likely get there quickly, but you probably wouldn't be able to repeat the route without the navigator. You took the easy way—no shame there, we all do it—but you wouldn't have learned how to repeat the drive.

If you used an old paper map instead, and chose the route that looked the most interesting, you probably would arrive at your destination a little later. You most likely would have taken some wrong turns, maybe had to backtrack a little, gotten stuck in some traffic. But your brain would have worked hard to find the destination—and as a result, you would likely have a much better sense of how you had gotten there.

It turns out that having your brain work hard is important. Learning is most effective when it requires effort. I can imagine you rolling your eyes as you read that, and thinking *Obviously*, but let me explain further. There is a principle called the desirable difficulty principle that was developed by a researcher named Robert Bjork. Dr. Bjork found that the harder your brain works to dig out a memory, the more learning that occurs (Bjork and Bjork 2014).

If you read that carefully, you would have noticed that I referenced digging out a memory. To dig something out implies that it has to already be there in order to be found. Which leads to the next crucial piece of learning: spreading out the learning. Revisiting what you've learned over and over again so as to reinforce it, so it really sticks.

When you first learn a concept, it's easy. You read it, you get it, it's good. But that is just surface learning; it isn't going to stick in your memory without more effort. If you learn something one day, and it's easy and good, and then the next day you try to remember (dig out) the memories from before, you're working much harder. It is this effort that creates greater learning in your brain. This is why it's so much more effective to study over time versus all at once.

Studying over time is not an intuitive skill; humans, for whatever reason, tend to want to put things off until the last minute. It would be great if this worked, but it doesn't. Creating a change, where you study bits over time, is a commitment, and having a visual schedule that you can reference can make a world of difference. Everyone does this differently—for some kids, this means a whiteboard hanging over their desk; for other kids, this looks like a wall of sticky notes that list each task they need to do. Sometimes you have to try out one method, and then try out another one, but making and sticking to a schedule helps with efficiency. And the more efficient you are at studying, the less time wasted, and the more time for doing the things you enjoy!

The research has repeatedly shown that to get your brain to work at full power, you need to repeatedly engage many different synapses. The best way to do this is to do more study sessions. They don't have to be hours long, but they do need to be spread out over time. If you find you struggle with keeping your study schedule at first, just be patient. Most of us wouldn't be able to run five miles after one jog, but if we put in time and effort and built our stamina slowly, eventually we'd be able to run five miles with ease. Same goes for studying.

Of course, we're often tempted to cut corners with studying and learning. You've probably had the experience of sitting down the night before a test to cram all the knowledge you're supposed to have into your brain in time for the test. You've probably also had the experience of quickly forgetting everything you crammed in after the test was done. It's understandable to want to study in this way, but you won't really be learning if you do. I'm sure you can remember moments where you quickly learned something, seemingly without effort, and couldn't even remember the topic the next day. For better or worse, learning requires effort.

BRAIN HACK: If a task or action takes less than two minutes, do it now.

David Allen, a productivity expert, came up with this two-minute rule as a formula for action. If you're thinking about making a study guide on a whiteboard, sketch it out now. If you remember you have something to add to the study guide, write it down right away. If the action takes less than two minutes, get it done right away so you don't forget it. Remember, learning takes effort, but forgetting is easy. Remembering what you need to learn is also crucial, and when you use the two-minute rule, you're bypassing the need to encode the task in your brain and using words to write it down and remember it. Two minutes or less? Do it now.

CRAMMING DOESN'T WORK—BUT THERE ARE THINGS THAT DO

If you cram, you will sort of learn the material, but you won't remember it over the long run. And you may pass the test you crammed for, but you probably won't pass the final unless you cram again. And if you do that, you won't ultimately hang on to anything you were supposed to learn. So it really doesn't make sense to keep cramming.

Psychologists have actually proved this with research. They found that our brain synapses encode (store) memories in our hippocampus much more effectively when we space out our learning. This spacing ensures that your brain has the time and ability to consolidate the information you are learning. When we cram, we engage only one set of our synapses, but when we space out our learning, multiple sets of synapses are used. Spacing out learning is like turning your brain's power fully on (Baudry et al. 2011).

So cramming doesn't work. But there are strategies that do work—that let you engage multiple synapses and really hold on to what you're learning. The basics—sleep, exercise, and nutrition—are the biggest of them all. Without these basics, your brain is unable to function at its highest level. This is important to keep in mind, as the strategies below will work best when your brain has time to consolidate the information you're learning, make new neural pathways, and is fully charged. In other words, sleep, exercise and nutrition are essential.

WHAT DOES WORK

Shake up your studying. Make your studying new and interesting each time. Remember how your gorgeous teen brain loves novelty (new things)?

It is easily bored, and quick to lose focus. Keep your studying varied and interesting. A landmark study by Dr. Steven Smith and colleagues found that when studying is varied, there is a slightly slower rate of remembering at first, but a much bigger amount of learning and skill over time (Smith, Glenberg, and Bjork 1978). Changing your physical environment can have an impact on your ability to remember new information. When you introduce your brain to novelty (something new, like a different room) your brain pays more attention to the information.

So, if you normally study at the kitchen counter, try using the dining room, the front porch, or even the local coffee shop. See if that changes how easy it is to understand and hang on to what you learn. The old advice was to study in a space with as little distraction as possible, and maybe the space you currently use has been set up for that. But the study found that when we learn information, it can help to study in different environments, so that you might find a place with a little background noise works too.

Vary the order in which you study. A lot of school involves learning things in the most logical order. This is, well, logical, but it's not always the most effective way of learning. Our brain gets too used to what we're looking at, and it isn't learning to be more flexible. For example, one study had students learn to identify different artists by looking at pictures those artists had painted. Traditionally, this type of learning is done by looking at a series of painting by the same artist. What the researchers found, however, is that students learned best when they looked at a wide variety of artists. The students were better able to identify the specific artist they were studying when they saw their work in the context of other painters' works—that is, when they had something novel they could compare the original artist's work and style to (Kornell and Bjork 2008).

Here are a couple of other ideas for shaking up your study practice. If you're using flash cards to study, don't keep them in the same order each time you review. When you make yourself tests or quizzes to pretest, switch up the questions and throw in some random ones that aren't really related to the topic at hand. Your brain needs to be ready for the unexpected, and it is built to pay special attention to things that are out of order or in the wrong place. When you mix up how you learn, your brain learns better.

Take good study breaks. If you're wondering whether there's research on the best way to benefit from study breaks, good news, there is! Generally, the research has shown that the ideal study break is twenty minutes or less. One kind-of-obvious point is that breaks that involve video games or social media, or are too long, often make it impossible to come back to your work.

In the very best case, a twenty-minute study break will involve either exercise or a short power nap.

Exercise during a study break is super-effective. Dr. Barbara Fenesi and colleagues did a study where they looked at types of study breaks, and how the study breaks impacted attention, short term learning, and long-term learning. They found that the teens who exercised during breaks performed better both on tests that day and on tests in the near future. The kids who exercised also reported that they felt they had better focus and understood more after their exercise break. The title of Dr. Fenesi's paper was appropriately named "Sweat So You Don't Forget" (Fenesi, 2018). Why not give it a try?

BRAIN HACK: Do jumping jacks during study breaks.

Yes, I'm serious. Cardio exercise has great research supporting its effectiveness for studying. If you use your breaks to get up, jump, dance, or otherwise get your heart rate going from exercise, you will be more effective when you return to your task. Your attention will have a boost, and your brain will think a little more clearly. Do one minute of jumping jacks, then one minute of break (anything but your phone!), and repeat this pattern four more times for a total of ten minutes. It really does make a difference. And if you're reluctant to try this one, do it for just a couple of minutes at a time.

Naps also help, but this is a tricky one. I know way too many teens who take long naps in late afternoon or evening, and then stay up late to do homework. This is a bad strategy. It messes up your sleep cycle and contributes to your always feeling tired. Naps should only happen before four p.m., and they shouldn't be longer than twenty minutes. If you can't take a nap using those guidelines, you're better off avoiding naps.

Short power naps (under twenty minutes and before four p.m.) do help with memory. Dr. Sara Mednick, a nap researcher, found that ten- to twenty-minute naps helped with memory, focus, and concentration. Naps seem to give your brain a soft reset. You wake up feeling more relaxed, less anxious, and more able to take in information (Mednick 2006).

Try setting smaller goals. If you're struggling to stay on task as you study, try setting small goals that you can get through in reasonable amounts of time. When your brain perceives that you're getting close to completing a task, it goes faster. In fact, the closer you get to meeting a goal, the harder you work and the faster you go. This is called the gradient theory, and it comes out of the work of a psychologist named Clark Hull. He initially did experiments with rats and saw that the closer they got to the cheese at the end of a maze, the faster they solved the maze (Hull 1938). The same has proven true with people. If we can trick ourselves into thinking we're almost done, our brains work harder and faster.

Avoid just reviewing notes over and over. Surprised? This is the number one way kids tell me they study. Just reading your notes over and over, like so many teens (and kids and adults) do isn't effective. This is more akin to cramming than anything else. Is there effort involved when you read your notes over? Do you start to tune out after a while? This type of learning is easy, feels logical—and just doesn't work. Remember: we want your brain to work. Your brain holds information and keeps it when it has to remember and think hard.

Rereading information involves pretty low stress and low effort. You aren't having to test yourself, and the answers are right in front of you. It's very easy in this situation to say to yourself, *Oh, I get this.* Rereading gives a false sense of security about learning and is one of the least effective learning strategies out there. Called the fluency illusion, it's exactly how we trick ourselves into believing that we know the information that is literally available to us and right in front of our face. Now, let's talk about something else that *does* work—testing yourself and giving your brain a challenge as you go over material you need to learn.

Test yourself. I know. This sounds awful, and, honestly, who wants to take more tests? Don't you do enough of that already? Unfortunately (or fortunately), this is one of the most effective learning strategies. Testing forces us to organize the material in our brain, and it changes how we think about that material.

Science writer Benedict Carey calls this technique pretesting. Pretesting helps you identify what you don't know, and it also makes your brain work harder to pull information out of your memory. And, as you now know, when your brain has to work to retrieve information, the information is more cemented in your hippocampus. Your brain synapses are able to strengthen the memory (Carey 2015).

There are several ways that testing yourself actually makes you learn more effectively. The first has to do with timing. The longer the delay between studying and testing, the better. As you know, cramming doesn't work because your brain forgets everything when it isn't reinforced. But if you test yourself a week before and then a few days before a test, you get a big advantage in learning (Halamish and Bjork 2011).

Testing yourself also helps if you can make sure to change up the language and style of the test. If you need to be able to understand and explain concepts, then just memorizing the vocabulary or set answers won't work. When you change up your approach, you're actually asking yourself questions about the material. You are moving the information around in your mind and thinking about it with different language. The more you do this, and the more effort you put into learning, the more the information sticks.

Testing yourself can be as simple as using flashcards and asking yourself what the meaning of a term is. Self-testing can be on an online quiz, the answers at the end of the chapter, or even a study guide. But once you have those questions down, you do need to ask them in different ways and with different words so you haven't simply memorized the question and answer. Remember, the effort of retrieving memories is the way we learn best. Don't make it too hard but also avoid making it too easy. You want to work your brain.

BRAIN HACK: Sleep between study sessions.

This can be another way of shaking things up while you study. When we sleep, our memories consolidate and become more firmly rooted in our brains. Research has shown that studying days ahead of things helps, both because the memory retrieval process makes the gains more solid and because the sleep allows the information to get well stored in the brain. For most teens, nine hours of sleep a night is a good amount to aim for.

Give and get positive feedback as you study and test yourself. Positive interactions with other people improve your performance. In one study, happiness researchers found that the quality of adults' work improved when there was a 3:1 ratio of positive to negative interactions. In fact, in the highest-performing work environments, there is a 6:1 ratio of positive to negative interactions. The researchers found that positive feedback leads to positive change. They even found that outside of work when people have three positive thoughts to each negative thought, they report being happier, more optimistic, and more fulfilled (Fredrickson and Losada 2005). Pretty cool, right? So, try going out of your way to support others and to allow yourself to be supported and complimented—especially when you're dealing with something difficult or challenging. You'll likely find that the more you practice giving positive compliments and feedback, the easier it will get, and the more positive compliments and feedback you receive, the easier the work you have to do will seem.

CHANGING STUDY PRACTICES IS POSSIBLE

Imagine you're sitting in class, and the teacher hands out a test. You take a look at the questions, and as you flip through the pages, you realize that you know this material. Some of the questions are asked in a tricky way, but that's okay. Your brain has stored this information. You learned over days instead of cramming, and you maximized your brain's ability to learn. What would that feel like? I imagine it would feel pretty good.

It's so hard to change how we do things, but it is also very possible to change how we do things. Your brain is ready and willing to do the work of changing how you study. There remain obstacles, of course, and one of the biggest obstacles to learning for teenagers is…procrastination. There are a ton of reasons why procrastination is such a big challenge for teens, from your brain makeup to the endless interesting information and experiences all around you. And, as much as you may want to put off reading the next chapter (all about procrastination), keep going! New strategies and skills to fight off the dreaded procrastination tendency are waiting.

CHAPTER 8

Procrastination: The Villain

I once heard an author who had written a book on procrastination describe it as his "most purchased and least read book." It made me laugh, especially because I owned the very book he was describing, and I had read only bits and pieces of it. If we procrastinate even on books about procrastination, then we're in trouble. The word itself comes from the Latin verb *procrastinare* which means "to put off until tomorrow." But, if you dig deeper, you get to the Greek word *akrasia,* also part of the origin of the word, and akrasia means "the state of mind in which someone acts against their better judgment through weakness of will."

Akrasia is where it gets interesting. "State of mind" refers to a temporary state—not something permanent. States of mind change. And if we can change our state of mind, does that mean we can get out of the habit of procrastinating? Yep. CBT and neuroscience will again lead the way.

Piers Steel, a researcher on procrastination, and a self-proclaimed procrastinator, clarifies that people don't procrastinate intentionally. Steel told the author of a *New Yorker* article, "One thing that defines procrastination isn't a lack of intention to work. It's difficulty following through on that intention." And this isn't a new thing. There are actual Egyptian hieroglyphics that read "Friend, stop putting off work and allow us to go home in good time." Procrastination has been around as long as humans, and it has interfered with our success throughout time (Konnikova 2014).

Adolescence, as you probably guessed, is a time when procrastination becomes even more challenging. It's the same problem we keep running into: the PFC just isn't fully connected yet. The PFC is crucial for productivity as it allows us to hold information in our minds and keep it accessible while we work with it. If we can't access information, it becomes very frustrating, making it easier to justify procrastinating.

Procrastination isn't even enjoyable. Teens tell me this all the time. They are busy avoiding doing work by using their phones or computers, but the thing they are supposed to be doing is always present. It's kind of like a cloud hanging over them. It would be one thing if they could just have a total blast distracting themselves, but the truth is that procrastination dulls the joy of whatever it is you're doing to avoid doing the actual thing.

When you procrastinate on studying or writing papers, you may eventually get them done, but in general, teens say the work they turn in or the studying they do isn't as good as it could have been. This just feels bad. As you're going to read in a couple of chapters, we all need a sense of meaning and purpose in our lives, and when we don't do the things that give us a sense of our own power and ability, it often feels terrible.

Teens and young adults report that procrastination is one of the biggest obstacles to their success. They describe feeling powerless against procrastination. And, while it's true that procrastination has a strong pull, you *can* resist it.

PROCRASTINATION AND THE TEEN BRAIN

The teen brain is a busy place. It is invested in social connections, feeling deeply, and finding new and novel experiences. You know this already, but these facts help us understand why procrastination is particularly tricky in the teen years. Again, your limbic system (the feeling part of your brain) has more power right now than it ever will again, and your PFC (the thinking part of your brain) is still not fully wired. So it makes sense that the effort of hard focus is more challenging right now, and that you just want to put it off. Your brain wants to feel good and is struggling with the motivation to endure boring tasks. If the limbic system is in charge, the emotions win out and procrastination is activated, but if the PFC can be reached, you can fight back.

If we never do things we don't like, life is pretty limited. The PFC is the boss. If we can get the PFC to understand the importance of the task, we will usually do it. But the problem is that the limbic system is yelling and screaming at the PFC to just ignore the task—it's going to feel bad or boring or uncomfortable—and the limbic system would like to avoid putting you through this negative experience. The limbic system is even sending out norepinephrine, which raises your levels of fear and anxiety, and the more fear it senses, the more you will making want to avoid.

Researcher Dr. Tim Pychyl describes procrastination as a problem of managing emotions rather than a time management issue (Sirois and Pychyl 2013). If the only thing we needed to do to stop procrastinating and start working was make a schedule, I think most of us would have little problem with procrastination. Instead, we focus more on avoiding bad feelings in the moment, rather than thinking ahead about how the procrastination will affect us later. And the teen brain is all about feeling good, so procrastination is especially challenging for teens.

I imagine the PFC as a coach or a teacher, and the limbic system as a tired, hungry, cranky kid. "But I don't want to!" is the phrase of the day. If the PFC can get past the whining and say, "Too bad. You need to do it anyway," we're in better shape. But how does the PFC really hear the information? We have to get the limbic system to both chill out and find some motivation. If we can convince the limbic system that there is benefit, we can change the message it sends to the PFC. And this is where CBT comes in. By changing our thoughts and our behaviors, we can change the messaging in our brain. Our limbic system can relay different emotions to the PFC, and we can motivate rather than just avoid and whine. As always, easier said than done, but still very possible.

Jen, age fifteen, is struggling with studying for a test in biology. She knows it would be better to do it sooner (she read the chapter on learning and knows that the more she does over time, the better her brain learns information), but she just hates doing the actual studying. Ironically, she actually likes biology, and she sometimes thinks she would like to have a career in the sciences. But when she goes to sit down and work, she can't get herself to do anything. She starts thinking about what she will have for dinner, the conversation she had with a friend the night before, or literally anything that pops in her mind. Her limbic system is saying "Don't study—it's so boring," and her PFC isn't getting the message to make her do the work.

First step: catch the thoughts. Jen notices what negative thoughts are going through her head about studying. Here are some of the automatic thoughts that she records:

Why bother? I'm not going to do well anyway.

I can only study when I'm stressed and the actual test is soon.

I'm scared I'm not smart enough to really understand this material.

BRAIN HACK: Prime your brain to study.

Remember brain priming? It's where we deliberately change our mood or state of mind. In a study published in 2013, researchers Dr. Sirois and Dr. Pychyl found that procrastination is about mood repair. In other words, as they explained, procrastination is much more about managing the mood you're feeling in the moment rather than allowing you to work toward your long-term goals. Don't make yourself feel guilty about not studying—it's not effective—but do make yourself feel excited about some aspect of the learning to come. Here's what this might look like:

Ineffective: "You can't get this done in time; there's no point in trying."

Effective: "This isn't going to be easy, but you're going to have to do it at some point. Get it done and then you get to relax without the guilt hanging over you. You got this."

When we do work, we're often acting toward a longer-term goal. If you start studying on Monday for a test that is on Friday, then you're motivated by the goal of doing well on Friday's test. Of course, it's not always easy to justify time on Monday for something that doesn't occur until Friday. And for some kids, it's really, really hard. Boys tend to struggle more with procrastination than girls, and teens who already fall further on the impulsive side also struggle more. In fact, impulsivity is related to procrastination. Dr. Steel, the procrastination researcher you read about earlier, has shown that procrastination is related to poor self-control, which is also a factor in impulsivity. Basically, impulsivity is acting when we should wait, and procrastination is waiting when we should act (Konnikova, 2014). And teens are one of the groups that struggle most with self-control, and therefore with impulsivity and procrastination.

Let's look at Mateo. Mateo is sixteen, and a self-described "crazy bad procrastinator." Mateo regularly waits until the last minute to do schoolwork, and he often stays up way too late on the night before it's due. He rushes to do the assignment in the least amount of time possible, and his grades reflect his procrastination. The few times he was able to follow the ideas laid out in Chapter 7, he got high marks. But when he reverts back to procrastination (no judgment, we've all done it) he suffers in both grades, sleep, and mood. But Mateo thinks there is no other way. "I can't make myself do it unless I know I have no other option."

You may remember that the basic idea of CBT is that it's not the situation that causes the problem, but rather it's how we perceive the situation that leads to the challenge. Mateo believes he cannot complete work unless he does at the last minute. His automatic thoughts support this belief. But, as you already know, our beliefs can be wrong. Let's see how you (and Mateo) can apply that point in real time to help get you out of the cycle of procrastination.

BRAIN HACK: Eat the frog.

Not literally (unless you want to). Eating the frog is an idea that came from the American writer Mark Twain. Mr. Twain said, "If it's your job to eat a frog, it's best to do it first thing in the morning. And if it's your job to eat two frogs, it's best to eat the biggest one first." If there's something very unpleasant you have to do, get it over with first thing in the morning. If you have to eat a frog, and you do it right away when you get up, it means you have an awful couple of minutes rather than an awful day. If we put off what we dread the most, we have to think and worry about it until we do it. If we just get the worst bit over with, we get the feeling of accomplishment from doing it and the relief from not having to think about it anymore.

ATTENTION IS LIMITED

If you had a glass of water and drank it all, it would be empty. I know, an uninspired example, but it's true. The glass would no longer hold water unless you refilled it. Attention is kind of the same. We only have so much at one time, and unless we refill it (more on that to come) we run out.

Another way of looking at this is to think of your attention like a flashlight. If you point a flashlight at an area or object, that area or object is lit up. You can see where the beam of light is pointed, and the area illuminated by the light appears bright and clear. The areas to the side of the light are still dark, but the targeted area is visible. It takes energy to keep the flashlight bright and focused on the specific area; the light won't stay as bright as the batteries get dim, and your hand will get tired from holding the light so still. Our ability to pay attention is similar. We can focus intensely for a while, but our attention will eventually waver. It takes a lot of effort to hold our attention on one area, and eventually, like the flashlight does, our attention weakens.

And when we run out of the ability to focus our attention, our brains are less able to filter out all the extra stimulation coming in from the world. You know when you're totally caught up in something and you lose track of time? You look up and might notice that it's gotten dark or started raining—all while you were focused on something else. In order to pay attention to that degree, the brain has to focus hard—it literally blocks out other conscious thoughts. When that attention runs out, suddenly there is all kinds of information from the world at hand flooding into your brain. It can be hard to figure out how to regain your focus and not get lost in all the distractions you're facing.

Mateo would tell you that he can totally pay attention when he is racing to finish work at the last minute. The flashlight is focused only on the task he is completing, and he keeps his eyes on the work. But attention does not last forever. So while Mateo may be able to use the stress response (remember the cortisol, norepinephrine, and adrenalin that are rushing through him) to keep himself on task, his level of focus will flicker.

As you know, work done in a serious rush and at the last minute is generally not the same quality as work done over time with revisions and remembering. Mateo, in his late-night cramming, is working with a flashlight that goes in and out. That turns off and on. He keeps shaking it and turning it to get at least some light, but the quality is less. His attention is running out, and his work quality is suffering as a result. But if he resists the temptation to procrastinate, sets up a schedule that allows him to learn and really handle the work he needs to do in a manageable way, and sticks with the commitments he makes in this schedule, he can keep his attention consistent and strong. And he can succeed. The most important component of Mateo's success will be his motivation. If he lets his thoughts shift to the negative and self-defeating, he will be fighting against his own limbic system. But, if he can remember the bigger why involved in the tasks he has to do, he will be more likely to change his thoughts to motivate his behavior.

Changing thoughts can help change behaviors. This is especially true with procrastination where our brain tries to trick us into giving up just because the limbic system doesn't want us to feel uncomfortable. Changing thoughts to increase motivation and have a sense of meaning or purpose can make a big difference in this situation. And there's more we can do to battle procrastination. We can also look at strategies to change behaviors. This is the full CBT picture: thoughts and behaviors.

DISTANCING THE DISTRACTIONS

Mateo told me, "I honestly could be distracted by a pencil." And while I believe that is true, I also know that for the most part, it's not a pencil that's causing the biggest distraction for Mateo. In reality, his biggest distractions come from electronics. By doing nothing more than making a few clicks on his phone, Mateo can play games on his phone, text with his girlfriend, and watch a video of a dog surfing. That is a high level of interest immediately available to him. And, as you know well, that's only the beginning of what he can do on his devices.

As a person who grew up well before cell phones and tablets, I can't even imagine the challenge of trying to focus on homework with all this fascinating material immediately available. In fact, even as an adult with a fully wired brain, I have to limit what's around me to avoid getting sucked into a vortex of ducks wearing costumes (which are seriously adorable). Dr. Steel has found that the closer we are to high-interest distractions, the more likely we are to procrastinate. "Proximity to temptation," he writes, "is one of the deadliest determinants of procrastination," and "the more enticing the distraction, the less work we do" (Steel 2011). In other words, if you're close to something you find interesting, you're more likely to procrastinate.

At the same time, we know from the chapter on learning that we don't want to study in a perfectly empty room with absolutely no noise at all. We need a little stimulation to help us focus. But what may be minimal distraction for me may be major distraction for you, and vice versa. Which leads to another insight: it's helpful to understand what distracts you the most so you can figure out what to do about it. For Mateo, it was his phone. He tried to tell himself he could resist it and not turn to it for a break, but when I asked him to track how often he used it, he realized he went to it far more often than he wanted to or realized.

Mateo has to literally put his phone in a different room, in a hard-to-reach place, with the volume turned off, to resist the temptation to check it and get sucked in by its distractions. And Mateo is not at all unusual. Most teens need this level of distance from their phones. This isn't a sign of weakness. In fact, that you're willing to take the steps you need to take to distance yourself is a sign of serious strength. Remember: the closer the temptation, the more likely you are to give in to it. And, if you can't put it away, plan for how to avoid the distraction. And once you've made that plan, stick to it. You'll see the rewards!

What's your plan? If you're anything like me, you just read the paragraph above and thought, *That's a great idea! I need to try that.* But then, when it's actually time to do it, you'll find some reason to keep your phone close. Maybe you're waiting for a text, or maybe you tell yourself that you'll put it away next time. It doesn't take much to find a good excuse for not following through. So let's make a plan now. Where is a place you can stash your phone that you will remember, where siblings won't find it, and where is a good distance from your study area? One teen I work with puts his phone in a basket under the bathroom sink. I tend to put mine on top of a tall cabinet. What place could you use? What's your plan for actually following through? Maybe a sticky note on your laptop reminding you? Or an index card propped up on the area you use for studying that reads "Phone Away!"?

In the epic poem *The Odyssey* (if you haven't read it yet, you will), the hero Odysseus has to take his boat past Sirens (beautiful creatures on the edge of a cliff) who sing so enchantingly that sailors jump out of the boat to try to swim to them. The Sirens intentionally lure sailors to jump out of the boat and inevitably drown. Knowing this, Odysseus had to prepare for their powerful and deadly distraction. He had his crew tie him to the mast and plug their own ears with wax so they couldn't hear the irresistible singing. Odysseus, knowing the power of the Sirens' song, physically restrained himself, and the crew literally blocked out the sound. Compared to what Odysseus did, putting your phone in a different room to avoid distraction seems like a small act, but it is, nonetheless, the same idea. You have to know what your temptations are and make sure those temptations are as inaccessible as possible.

Odysseus is trying to make it home after a long time at war. His goal is to get home safe and sound, so it is worth it to be tied to a mast. Mateo wants to get a good grade in his class to boost his GPA. Mateo dreams of becoming a civil rights attorney, and he knows the first step is going to college. Both Odysseus and Mateo have long-term goals that make their efforts of avoiding distraction worthwhile.

The next step to managing procrastination is figuring out what it is you're working toward. What are your goals? Let's explore those now.

WHICH GOALS MOTIVATE YOU?

Procrastination is easy. Hard work is, well, hard. When you have to do something that takes effort and focus, it takes a lot of work from your brain. Your limbic system is fighting for control from your PFC, and it's looking for distractions and entertainment. It can be hard to keep your brain focused on the task at hand, and you need all available strategies to help. Removing your distracting temptations is a starting point, but now, the next step is to look at what personally motivates you to do this task; that's what will help you commit to keeping up on it. What is the bigger goal for completing this task?

Mateo was working to improve his GPA to get into college. Odysseus had the bigger goal of survival. Your goals may be closer to Mateo's or as big and serious as Odysseus's. Regardless, having a goal that the work you do will contribute to uses both your PFC and limbic system—it gives you a little emotional boost ("I want this!") while calling on your thinking and planning brain as well, as you keep figuring out the steps to make your goal.

Take a minute to list five goals right now. Don't overthink it; just come up with five things you really want to achieve. You might include broad goals like having a successful career that you love or specific goals like traveling to Japan to see the moss gardens in Kyoto. It's okay if some of the goals you write down seem silly or out there. Totally fine. We're going to dig into goals and how they relate to your sense of purpose a little further in the book, but for right now we simply want some goals that will motivate you.

Once you have some goals written down, think about how the work you're doing every day right now might contribute to those goals. If you're sitting at the kitchen table, staring at your homework, and the siren song of your phone is calling to you, it can help to have something bigger to focus on. "I just need to get through this chapter and study. This test matters for my grade, and I have a real chance to boost my class grade if I do well on this. And if I can do that, I'm one step closer to having Mom and Dad take me on that trip to Japan to see the moss gardens. I can do this." Your CBT skill of catching and evaluating your thought patterns will help you figure out when you're starting to get distracted and procrastinate. And when you catch yourself starting to slip into distraction, a small pause to remind yourself of your goal can help you resist the procrastination pull and refocus on what needs to get done.

Mateo wants to be a civil rights attorney someday. This is his big goal. He knows he needs his limbic system and his PFC onboard to help him work toward this goal so he screenshots a picture of his hero, Martin Luther King Jr., and uses it as wallpaper on his phone. Every time he unlocks his phone, he looks at a picture of Dr. King, and sometimes that's enough to get him to put down his phone and go back to his work.

BRAIN HACK: Set up a reminder of your goal to keep yourself on track.

You might follow Mateo's lead and find some way to set up a visual reminder of your goal in a prominent place—like on your phone, or on a bedroom mirror, or on the cover of your planner where you can see it every day—to keep it at the top of your mind, especially when you're tempted to procrastinate more than you should.

Big goals help us have a broader sense of motivation. They can also feel kind of distant sometimes. They may even be a bit daunting to consider. In fact, they can be so big that they steer you to procrastination too. So, we also need to look at ways we can break down our big goals into smaller goals, to keep us on track and help us move forward in a way that feels real and possible. I'm sure you've heard the saying that a journey of a thousand miles begins with a single step. Let's try to break up your big goal and make it easier to attain. Baby steps ahead.

START SMALL AND CHUNK IT OUT

First, apologies for the word "chunk." It's unpleasant, but it's necessary here to describe what needs to happen. Right now, you have some skills for catching yourself when you start to procrastinate and getting yourself back on track. You understand the basics of procrastination, you're making temptation hard to access, you're engaging your limbic system with a bigger goal. And now we need to make it even easier for your PFC to focus. You're going to break down your goals into smaller steps, or chunk them out.

Forget about Odysseus here. His epic journey home is no longer going to be as useful; let's focus instead on Mateo. Mateo wants to become a civil rights attorney. That's his big goal. What are the smaller goals he needs to achieve in the long run, medium run, and short run? He has a long-term goal of law school. That means he needs to graduate from high school with good enough grades (and experiences, like extracurriculars) to get into college. So, he has a medium-term goal of graduating with a 3.6 GPA or above. In order to achieve that goal, he has a short-term goal of getting all As and Bs this semester. Make sense? You already listed big goals; now make it a little more specific. What are your long-term, medium-term, and short-term goals?

And once you have those goals written out, it's time to chunk out even further. What specifically needs to happen for you to make your shortest-term goal? In order for Mateo to get all As and Bs this semester, he will need to use the learning strategies from Chapter 7 to plan out his studying. Sounds good, but you have to remember that Mateo is the same kid who said he could be distracted by a pencil. So it's going to be a little tougher for him to resist procrastination. Tougher, but not impossible.

His first step is to catch his automatic thoughts, which so often steer him to procrastinating behaviors. He starts to track them and realizes that he is frequently saying things to himself like, "You work better when you're stressed" or "You can't do this; you're not capable of focusing." As he tracks his thoughts, he sees a pattern that enables (even encourages) procrastination. Once he recognizes this pattern, Mateo starts to work on deliberately changing his automatic thoughts. This isn't easy or natural, but when he catches the negative thoughts, he starts to say to himself, "Mateo, you got this. You can do hard things." He even writes this down on an index card and puts it on his bathroom mirror. He repeats it to himself when he looks in the mirror. And when he catches himself thinking things like *I work better when I'm stressed,* he questions those thoughts: *Is it absolutely true that I wouldn't work better if I gave myself time to finish my assignments without rushing? I'm not sure I've really given that a shot yet. Let's find out.*

The next step is to further chunk out projects so he can start to adjust his work pattern away from procrastination. If Mateo has a big test on a Wednesday, he comes up with a plan that involves twenty minutes of studying a day, starting a full week before. He keeps the studying to twenty minutes because, as he says, "I can do almost anything for twenty minutes. No excuses." If he had told himself he had to study for an hour each day for the week leading up to the test, how likely would he have been to actually do it? Not very. He would have gotten overwhelmed, his limbic system would have sent him all kinds of feelings, and he would have gone back to staring at a pencil rather than doing work.

BEYOND PROCRASTINATION

In this chapter, we discussed strategies for avoiding procrastination. Start small. Change your thoughts to challenge the negative automatic thoughts that encourage you to give up (thanks, limbic system). Change your behaviors that make it easy to procrastinate by moving your phone and other distractions far away when you need to concentrate. Have a bigger goal in mind—a reason for what you're doing. Use your learning strategies. And now that you've got these new skills, you may want to amplify your gains. The next chapter is about meditation and mindfulness, two strategies that make learning and living a little easier. You'll learn more ways to manage your mood and calm your mind.

CHAPTER 9

Meditation and Mindfulness

Do the words "meditation" and "mindfulness" bring up images of someone sitting cross-legged, wearing white robes and chanting "Ommmm"? If so, that's totally okay. It's not a wrong image, but it's also not a complete image. Meditation and mindfulness have been around for centuries, and there's a reason for that. They work. You may be surprised to know there are research studies that support meditation and mindfulness for everything from stress management, improved emotional regulation, increased compassion, and a reduced automatic reaction to attractive food. There is one study that even finds mindfulness reduces prejudice against different races and ages (Lueke and Gibson 2014).

WHAT'S ALL THE HYPE?

Stereotypes, like the image of the yogi chanting, sometimes make it easier for us to dismiss an idea by making it seem invalid or sketchy. I'm always surprised by how easy it is to let myself go along with a stereotype rather than really exploring and questioning what I'm seeing. What is clear, and beyond any stereotype, is that teens who meditate and/or practice mindfulness experience positive brain changes that increase their ability to think more and react less.

As you already know, you have the ability to change your brain. In fact, your brain is changing just by learning about how your brain changes. And if you picked up another skill, like learning to play the guitar, you would start building new neural pathways for that. The same is true with meditating—only meditating actually gives you more ability to stay in control and focus. It's like a skill that helps you better practice the skill of practicing and learning.

And research is showing this in fMRI studies of teen meditators. For example, one recent study found that adolescents who practiced meditation had clear increases in their gray matter. They also had greater development in the limbic system, the area of your brain where your emotional awareness lives (Yuan et al. 2020).

Learning to meditate and use mindfulness allows you to be better at managing your own emotions and understanding others' emotions. That is a seriously important skill for a teenager. As you already know, teens' brains are more reactive and more emotional. This is a tool that is free, easy to learn, and requires only fifteen or twenty minutes a day. What's not to like?

I'm guessing (or at least really hoping) that you're excited about the power of meditation and mindfulness. Meditation is a practice you do to hone a certain way of being and a certain way of paying attention. Mindfulness is a particular way of experiencing whatever you encounter in any given moment without judging it. They're both practices, things you literally learn and practice. In this chapter, we will look at them as two different ideas, but keep in mind that they are closely related.

MEDITATION

Meditating is the act of focusing on breath, a word, or an image in order to reach a different state of consciousness or being. Some people describe this state as peace; others talk about feeling connected to the world; still others focus on the benefits attaining a state of serenity can have for your awareness of yourself and your ability to be and act with calm and ease in your day-to-day life.

Ultimately, the goal of meditation is to move out of the chaos of the moment and into a space that's more centered. Sound appealing? Imagine if you could calm your mind when it was freaking out, completely irrational, or just feeling like everything was terrible. That actually can happen.

After you meditate for a bit, your brain learns to calm down, and the limbic system (home of the fight, flight, or freeze response) is more relaxed. FMRI studies show that teens who meditate regularly are more able to respond rather than just react. Teen meditators are less driven by their limbic system and more driven by their frontal cortex (Sanger and Dorjee 2015). In other words, you get to think before you just react out of emotion.

Meditation is a practice. If you want to get better at basketball, you practice dribbling and shooting; if you want to get better at meditating, you practice meditating. Some people choose to do formal meditation training programs to get this practice, like one teenager I worked with, Cathy. She had read about the research on meditation, and she wanted to try it out. I have seen meditation help many kids, but none as much as Cathy. When Cathy meditates, you can tell. She is visibly calmer and better able to deal with conflicts that come up, and she will tell you she feels much more confident and comfortable. Cathy learned a type of meditation that focuses on a single word, called a mantra. But meditation often starts by simply focusing on your breath.

Not everyone has a response as strong as Cathy's, and not everyone needs to go through a whole meditation training program. You can learn how to meditate from YouTube or books, and you can commit to practicing so that your meditation becomes routine. In my experience, kids who stick with meditating for a week or so, even for just a few minutes a day for a couple of weeks, have some type of response. They report changes that include feeling like they can concentrate more, feeling more content, and feeling more in control of their emotions.

I've included some basic steps as a guide on how to meditate, but you can also google "how to meditate" and you'll be amazed at what you come up with. Just remember to keep it simple. You don't need fancy cushions and bells. You just need a few minutes and a quiet space.

HOW TO MEDITATE

My basic steps for meditation come from the work of Joseph Goldstein, a world-renowned meditation teacher. He makes meditation simple and doable. Mr. Goldstein says, "If you're sitting and feeling the breath…and connecting with the breath, and then your mind wanders and … you see that, and you come back [to your breath]. No matter how many times you do that, you're doing [meditation] right" (Harris 2019). Basically, if you're sitting and focused on your breath, you're meditating. It's okay if your mind wanders while you meditate; just notice it when it wanders, and pull your focus back to your breath.

Set a timer with a gentle ringtone for anywhere between three and five minutes. (We're starting small.)

Get comfy. Sitting is best, and it can be on a chair, on the floor, or wherever you're comfortable. Mr. Goldstein recommends sitting in a "dignified" posture, which means a posture that honors the work you are doing. Try to sit up straight (but not in an uncomfortable way), and to hold your head up. You are practicing something important, and your body reflects that importance.

Settle into the sitting position. Gently close your eyes. Notice your body. Notice where it feels relaxed and where it doesn't. Focus in on the tense areas and slowly work to relax them.

Notice your breathing. Notice how the air comes in, notice how your stomach and chest rise and fall. Notice the exhalation. Don't change your breathing; just notice your own natural breathing rhythm.

When you notice yourself becoming distracted, just gently pull your thoughts back to your breathing. It's absolutely fine that you were distracted. That's normal and natural. Just bring your thoughts back to your breath.

Keep breathing. When the timer goes off, slowly open your eyes and bring your attention back to the room. Don't rush to jump up; take your time adjusting to the light and being aware of your surroundings.

And that's it. Meditation is most effective when you have a regular practice, and daily meditation is best. If you can practice for five minutes a day for a week, and then build up to ten minutes, and then maybe to fifteen, you're on your way. Most people find it works best to choose a regular time of day to practice so that it becomes routine. First thing in the morning, right when you wake up, or before you go to bed at night tend to be times that work well. It's okay if you miss a day too; forgive yourself, and meditate the next day.

MINDFULNESS

Mindfulness is being fully aware of the present moment without judging it. Mindfulness involves bringing your mind and your body together. For example, if you're eating cereal and playing a game on your phone, you're probably not really tasting or enjoying the cereal. In fact, your mind is likely far away from the act of eating and much more focused on the game you're playing. Before you know it, the cereal is gone, and you can't remember actually eating it.

Mindfulness involves paying attention to right now. This moment. This sounds simple, but it is often seriously hard. As I was writing this, I was trying to practice being mindful of my environment, and the tea I was drinking. I was trying to just drink the tea without judgment. But my first thoughts were judgments: *This could use a little more sugar* and *It's so warm* and *I wonder if this is going to wake me up a bit.*

Judgment is so much a part of our lives that it is challenging to experience things without judgment. Judgment isn't always negative; we may be making good judgments, like about how good the tea tastes once the level of sugar is right. But when we make judgments of any kind, we're inevitably seeing things in one way. And, as you know, things aren't usually just one way.

Here's an example: Spencer doesn't like Josh. He has known Josh since second grade, and all through elementary school, Josh would do stupid and hurtful things—Spencer thought he was a jerk. Now that they're older, though, Spencer is trying to practice being mindful, and he finds himself focusing on it while he's walking through the hallway at school. Josh calls out to him, and Spencer quickly loses his mindful state and thinks *What does he want? This kid is so annoying.* He walks away from Josh. He doesn't even acknowledge him.

There is so much going on in our minds all the time: school assignments, friend drama, family, and more. It's hard to focus on the moment we're in. Our brain is constantly feeding us information about the past, the future, our fears, and our obligations. Spencer's brain reminded him that he found Josh annoying, but if Spencer had been in the moment, able to separate himself from his automatic judgments, he would have seen that Josh's face looked sad. He might have noticed that Josh's voice sounded different as he called out to Spencer. He would have realized that Josh was uncomfortable, and he could have responded differently. He could have shown kindness or compassion.

Mindfulness has a strong connection with kindness and compassion. In fact, people who are less mindful tend to be more negative. Harvard researchers did a study where they checked in with people throughout the day and asked them to describe their thoughts at the moment of check-in. The scientists found that about half of the time most people were lost in their thoughts and not focused on the moment going on around them. And, the research found, the more a person's mind wanders, the more it tends to move toward negativity, anxiety, jealousy, anger, regret, and self-criticism (Killingsworth and Gilbert 2010).

If most of us are lost in our thoughts much of the time, and if getting lost in our thoughts means we tend to go down paths that lead us to more negative thoughts, then it makes sense that mindfulness can make us feel happier. It pulls us out of feeling bad about the past and scared about the future, and helps us focus on this moment. Right now.

So, if pulling out of feeling bad and really entering the present moment sounds like something you want—and most of us do—how do you become more mindful? Mindfulness is often described as paying attention on purpose, with deliberation. You've done this before. You know when you're struggling to pay attention to someone and you force yourself to really listen to what they're saying. That is mindfulness: being fully present in the very moment we're in. It's pretty cool.

Here are some basic steps to mindfulness:

Take a deep breath in through your nose and let it out through your mouth.

Notice your body—your feet on the ground, your bottom and back on your chair. Feel the surface that supports your body.

Notice any feelings that you're currently experiencing. Try not to judge the feelings; instead, notice them and name them—*I am feeling worried because of the test today.*

Allow yourself to feel the feeling. Invite the worry in. Experience it, and then let it go. Imagine the feeling is a cloud slowly moving across the sky. It is less and less visible.

A lot of teens I know like practicing mindfulness. It feels good, and they enjoy being in the moment. The problem they run into is that they forget to practice. It's not that they don't want to practice, but all the noise in their head takes over and they forget. That's okay. That's why we're doing this in in the first place! Here are a few strategies to help you remember to practice mindfulness:

Write yourself an encouraging sticky note that you change and move around as your practice of mindfulness evolves. The sticky note might read something like: "Be mindful. Take a breath and notice this moment." The first day it's on the mirror in your bathroom, the second day it's on your closet door. The third day, you rewrite it, with a new color sticky note; it now reads: "Stop. Take a moment, right now, to be mindful of this moment." After two more days, you change the colors and the message and location again—and you keep going, checking to see how your mindfulness habit is progressing.

Make your mindfulness a daily commitment tied to something you do regularly. For example, every time you wash your hands you will remember to breathe and be fully present in the moment. The easiest way to have success with this strategy is to write down the behavior you are linking with mindfulness each morning. As you're eating breakfast, make a note on an index card or on your phone that says something like "I will focus on mindfulness every time I sit down."

A bracelet or watch you wear regularly can also serve as a reminder to be mindful. Switch from the wrist where you usually wear the watch or bracelet, and every time you go to look at the time or feel the bracelet, there will be a little jolt of "Wait, what?" that reminds you to be mindful. If you don't normally wear a watch or bracelet, tie a piece of string loosely around your wrist or wear a rubber band. It's a little cue you will periodically notice throughout the day that can remind you to practice mindfulness.

A PLACE TO START

Richard Davidson, a professor at the University of Wisconsin, has spent his career studying the effects of meditation and mindfulness on health and happiness. Because of Davidson's efforts, the school even has a full-time mindfulness coach as part of their athletics department; they take mindfulness and meditation seriously. And they have the research to prove the benefits.

Davidson's research shows that learning mindfulness and meditation increases participants' overall well-being. When he talks about meditation and mindfulness, he is quick to mention that Americans are in an epidemic of loneliness and depression. And the data he uses to show the high rates of depression and loneliness all predate the COVID-19 pandemic. So how do we use meditation and mindfulness in our lives more regularly? We practice and practice and practice (Dahl, Wilson-Mendenhall, and Davidson et al. 2020).

A fourteen-year-old I know, Kara, was very excited about the idea of mindfulness. I explained the basics to her, and she rushed out and bought several books on the topic. But she didn't read the books, and as much as she liked the idea of mindfulness, it was hard for her to actually put it into practice. *I can't remember, I get distracted,* and *I love the idea, but I just don't have time* were some of the thoughts she shared that interfered with her practice. I've been there. I commit to an idea, I love the idea, but I never quite get around to putting it into practice. I think most of us have had this experience, and when it happens, we often have to regroup and start smaller.

Kara and I looked at the thoughts she had collected, and we used them as data points for where she struggled. Once the day got going, it was hard to make time for mindfulness, and she often simply forgot. Understandable. Instead of expecting herself to practice throughout the day, she changed the expectation to one time a day. She decided to practice mindfulness right away when she woke up. Knowing that she was still likely to forget, she put a sticky note over her phone when she went to bed, with the word "MINDFULNESS" in all caps on the front. When she woke up in the morning, she knew the first thing she would do would be to reach for her phone, and this note jolted her back to her goal.

Kara began to practice mindfulness first thing when she woke up in the morning. The sticky note worked! She used her mindful time in the morning to set an intention for the day. Once she woke up, she got out of bed and got comfortable in a nearby chair. She took three long deep breaths, in through her nose and out through her mouth, and then she focused on the day ahead. She asked herself, *What is my hope for today?* Kara was asking herself to focus on how she wanted to act that day—how to be the Kara she truly was inside.

After a few weeks of practicing each morning, Kara noticed themes in her intentions. She regularly wanted to be kind to herself, to be forgiving of others, and to be fully invested in the present moment. The morning practice started to spread, and without even realizing it, she found herself taking the three deep breaths at different points during the day and reminding herself: *Be kind and loving to myself. Be forgiving of others. And focus on this moment right now, pulling my thoughts back when they move too far ahead or behind.*

Kara's life did not become suddenly perfect or easy, but she did find a greater sense of calm and trust in herself. She felt a little more in control of her emotions, and she noticed that she enjoyed experiences a little more. She also was able to catch her negative voice, the one that always told her she wasn't good enough, and to challenge that negative voice a bit more. She didn't fight it, but she did remind herself to be kind and loving to herself. And, more often than not, it worked.

MEDITATION AND MINDFULNESS IN REAL LIFE

Our culture is not based on the ideas of meditation and mindfulness; in fact, it seems like the world is actively fighting against being in the moment, focusing on the breath, and accepting ourselves as we are. If you look at how many times we check our phones, compare our posts to other people's, or worry about the next thing we have to get done, it's easy to see how hard life makes it to slow down and be in this moment.

It takes time, effort, and practice to bring meditation and mindfulness into your life. But it is possible to practice these ancient skills and make them part of your day. Meditation and mindfulness have strong research supporting their effectiveness in a myriad of ways from concentration to overall happiness. And, unlike some things that are annoying or boring to learn, these are skills that actually feel good to learn.

When you are able to be more in the moment, rather than racing around in all directions, you can focus more on your intentions—how you want to be in the world. Practicing meditation and mindfulness can move you toward more interest in your sense of meaning in the world. The next chapter focuses on just that: creating a sense of personal meaning.

CHAPTER 10

Why Am I Doing All This? Finding Meaning

Meaning is one of the pillars of a good life. We all want to feel like we matter, and that our time on earth makes a difference. Meaning is what we think and feel inside ourselves; it is the idea we move to, and the hope we hold on to. Purpose is the bigger plan for how we create meaning. Meaning and purpose matter a great deal in your teen years. Most adolescents are actively seeking to have an impact, to create change, and to make the world better. It's not a coincidence that some of the biggest social change movements from the Vietnam era to the modern day gun violence protests have been driven by teenagers. You have a sense of power and agency, and you're able to work together to make real differences in the world.

It turns out that when we have a sense of meaning and purpose, we do better. What's more, meaning and purpose take on a new, special importance in adolescence. Right now, your frontal cortex is becoming developed enough to allow you to have big, deep thoughts about the meaning of life. When you were younger, any time you had these "higher level" thoughts, you would not only activate your frontal lobes but also your amygdala. The thoughts were always highly tinged with intense emotion. As you move later into your teen years, you get to have the big thoughts without the constant roller coaster of emotions; it becomes a more subtle but still powerful experience. As a teen, you're also more and more able to actually act on these big, deep thoughts about the meaning of life and what you want your life to be about.

Finding a purpose and committing to your meaning can be both liberating and scary. It can feel uncomfortable to make yourself vulnerable enough to say what really matters to you. Some kids I know fear that they won't be able to follow through on what they say they will do or live by and feel too worried about the potential embarrassment. Other kids are afraid their ideas will be judged as weird or stupid. An irony of adolescence is that just as you're becoming most passionate and committed toward your life and what you want it to be, you're also at the point where you most fear others' judgments.

Your experiences with CBT and mindfulness have probably taught you, though, that the ways we tend to judge things aren't always accurate. And pursuing the things that are meaningful to you actually is more important than the ways you might be judged by other people. Not just because of your belief in this greater thing, but also because when you have a sense of meaning that informs what you do, you typically end up feeling better and performing better. The research on this is very clear. Teens who have a stronger sense of meaning feel better about themselves, are less bored, are less likely to become depressed, are less likely to abuse alcohol or drugs, and are more likely to report a sense of happiness and well-being (Bronk 2014). Teens who have a sense of meaning even sleep better (Kim, Hershner, and Strecher 2015).

OUR SEARCH FOR MEANING ISN'T NEW

One of the first people to study how meaning impacted our lives was Viktor Frankl. Dr. Frankl was a psychiatrist who survived the concentration camps. He wrote *Man's Search for Meaning,* a book that you (hopefully) will read at some point. In this book, he talks about how he was able to endure the horrors of Auschwitz by having a greater sense of meaning and purpose about his own life.

Dr. Frankl describes walking to his forced labor in the bitter cold, without shoes or clothing beyond rags; he was starving and in terrible pain. But in his mind he imagined himself in a warm lecture hall speaking to a group of colleagues about the very experience he was then going through. The speech he was giving in his mind was about how he survived. Dr. Frankl believed that "those who have a 'why' to live, can bear with almost any 'how'" (Frankl 2019).

I recently shared this story with a teen I work with, and she responded, "I can't imagine what he went through, but I do the same thing. Only it's not nearly as hard as it must have been for him." When I asked her what she meant, she said that when she is overwhelmed she consciously chooses to find a sense of meaning in what she is doing. This helps guide her forward.

"My first semester at college was rough," she continued. "I kept getting sick. There was all kinds of drama with friends, and I felt overwhelmed. I wanted to go home. But then I thought about what I want to do when I get out of school. So much of my meaning is about helping other people, and I thought telling them the story of how I got through my first semester of school when I wanted to give up might actually be meaningful for someone else."

She changed her situation by changing how she thought about it. And, by adding meaning and purpose to her experience, it became more possible to get through it. It didn't become easy, but now there was a reason why she needed to push through.

What about you? When you think about your purpose, what words come to mind? Try not to censor yourself here; just notice what comes up in your mind when you ask yourself *What is my purpose?* And whatever comes up, keep in mind that it doesn't have to be one thing, and it doesn't have to make total sense. It can be helpful to think about what your purpose is at various points of time. How you think about it may change over time, or it may stay completely consistent; either way, it's totally okay. But you do have a purpose, and it's pretty cool to imagine what that will be.

Our brains respond to meaning. When we're living in a way with purpose and meaning, not only are the reward centers of our brain more activated but we also have better health. A recent study looked at happiness without meaning and happiness with meaning, and found that people who had a higher sense of meaning in their life actually had higher immune responses than those who just had happiness alone (Fredrickson et al. 2013). So it seems that meaning provides both increased physical health and increased mental health.

That said, meaning is not the same thing as happiness. At the same time, people who have a sense of meaning in their lives do report being happier overall. Let's take a closer look at the distinction between these two concepts. It's worth understanding this so you can cultivate a sense of meaning that really sustains you, whatever you end up facing in life. Meaning can serve as a compass. We all get lost, but meaning helps us find our way back to the path we have chosen. Meaning is something that sustains us; it's the bigger purpose that keeps us going in good times and bad.

MEANING VS. HAPPINESS

Which would you prefer: meaning or happiness? The answer I expect would be "Both!" I frequently ask teens what they think is the difference between meaning and happiness. It's not an easy question, and it can take a minute or two to answer. Generally, though, teens see happiness as more personal and situational. When they are happy, it is usually because they are doing something they like (eating something delicious, listening to a great song, hanging with a person they love) or something similar. In their description, meaning is like a backdrop that informs your life events and contexts, whether or not those are happy in any given moment. It tends to be more about a greater sense of purpose for their life, and about doing something to help others and to make a difference in the world. I think this description is about right.

In fact, Dr. Frankl believed that the pursuit of happiness was not a worthwhile or realistic goal. Happiness, Frankl believed, was a byproduct of our sense of meaning. What's more, "it is the very pursuit of happiness," Frankl explains, "that thwarts happiness" (Frankl 2019).

Interestingly, an eminent Harvard University professor of philosophy, Robert Nozick, had the same idea. Dr. Nozick was deeply interested in the ideas of happiness and meaning, but he wasn't sure that we were supposed to be happy all the time. He believed that meaning created a more fulfilling life (Nozick 1974).

Dr. Nozick designed a thought experiment (a way to try out a belief through an imaginative exercise) to explain this theory. He asked participants to imagine they could live in a tank that would give them any experience they desired. In this tank, you would be floating around, and your brain would be hooked up to some type of machine that made everything possible. You could travel, fight wars, win Oscars or Grammys; anything you wanted could exist in your mind. Would you choose this life rather than a regular life with all its ups and downs?

Most people don't choose to live in the tank despite the promise of constant happiness. People feel like it's not a real life and that they didn't earn those happy experiences so they count less.

Dr. Nozick writes: "There's more to life than feeling happy. Happiness without meaning characterizes a relatively shallow, self-absorbed or even selfish life, in which things go well, needs and desire are easily satisfied, and difficult or taxing entanglements are avoided." In other words, while it's not bad to have and seek happy moments in your life, the pursuit of happiness alone can lead to a smaller life than you might really want. And your life will be richer if you embrace life's stresses and ups and downs as much as you embrace its moments of happiness. Having a sense of the meaning and purpose of your life can help you do this.

FINDING YOUR MEANING

So what is your greater meaning or purpose? Meaning is different for everyone, but the general idea is that you're using your own skills and strengths to help others—people, animals, the planet, and more; to make a positive difference in the world. There are multiple parts to meaning, and researchers disagree on some of them, but the main components are a sense of involvement with something that is bigger than yourself, a sense of belonging and connectedness to the goal, and a commitment to or belief in the things you do as you're working toward your meaning.

In my practice, I have the privilege of talking with kids about meaning on a regular basis. A seventeen-year-old I know finds his meaning in being outside and creating environmental change. He is a devoted outdoorsman, and he finds that when he is actively working outside, planting trees, building trails, or beautifying areas, life feels meaningful. This meaning helps him as he thinks about the future. For him, the idea of an office job in a cubicle is terrifying. And as he sits through class after class in high school, he holds his meaning close. He knows that if he can get through high school and get to college he can study the environment, and he can be outside. He knows that if he has weekends full of outside time, he can hold on to that when the weekdays get boring. His meaning, creating environmental change through his work in nature, sustains him when he feels overwhelmed with the dullness of school.

Another teen I work with, a boy who is also seventeen, finds his meaning in writing. He is an eloquent poet, a short story and fan fiction writer. He finds math and science classes challenging, but he knows that he can express himself through his words and his characters, and he holds on to his greater meaning as he tackles equations and science labs. His life is not only about the difficult work he is doing now; he knows that this work will lead to his bigger goal of writing. Science may not directly relate to writing, but learning science leads to a diploma, which leads to opportunities that lead to writing.

This young man finds meaning in using words to create expression, feeling, and change. He uses his experiences in science and everywhere as tools for his writing, and he changed how he viewed the parts of his life he didn't like. Rather than seeing them as useless, he now actively works to think of them as (1) a necessary stepping-stone to a bigger goal, and (2) material and experience for his writing. By changing how he views science and math, he makes them more bearable and more relevant. His dream is to be a writer, and the funny part of it is that it isn't a dream at all—he's already a writer. He writes daily, and he finds that to be an anchor, a way of connecting him to what he loves when the world around him doesn't feel so good.

Try this yourself. Take a moment to think of a class, obligation, or chore that you really dislike. What is it that you most dislike about the experience? Write down your answer. Now, think about the parts that make up the experience that causes you so much distress. If you were to flip these parts or this experience to find the benefit, what would it be? I remember reading a book called *The Blessing of a Skinned Knee* when my kids were little. The author asks what you find to be your child's most annoying trait. I immediately thought of whining. She then asks you to flip that to a strength. It took me a minute—how could whining be a strength?— but then I got it. Whining is persistence. A kid who whines is trying very hard to get what they want. Obviously it's not a tactic that will work as they get older, but if their worst trait is whining, that could actually be a harbinger of a person who knows how to stick with something to get what they want. See how it works?

Now to the fun part. What are your strengths? List them on a piece of paper. It may feel awkward or uncomfortable, but there is nothing wrong with owning your strengths. If you want, you can tear up the paper when you're done. I'd rather you didn't—I'd like to see you hang it up high on your mirror—but regardless, get those strengths down on paper.

If you're feeling stuck, start by asking adults you care about what they see as your strengths and what they think you may contribute to the world. Of course, it's uncomfortable and awkward to do this, but honestly, most adults love this kind of thing. We're happy to be asked and to share our thoughts.

Once you have a sense meaning that feels real and useful to you, start taking a few minutes each day to visualize how you can add meaning to this day. When you focus on your sense of meaning, you're not only making it more likely you'll act on your meaning. You are also literally building up your own immune response system—making yourself stronger and healthier.

Imagining your meaning and beginning to make it more real so that it changes your thoughts and behavior actually changes your brain. When you consciously help others, the dorsal anterior cingulate cortex, a part of your brain that helps you with emotion management and attention, and part of your amygdala both have reduced stress activity, and you feel good from increased activity in your ventral striatum. A 2016 study using fMRIs showed that the people helping others had the clear gains. The people receiving the help had none of the changes (Inagaki et al. 2016). And the benefits go even further. When you help others not only do you feel good, but you also start a feedback loop where they are going to be more likely to help you and to think highly of you. This increases what's known as *prosocial behavior*.

BRAIN HACK: Keep your meaning in mind as you make decisions in the day-to-day.

Living by your personal sense of meaning is not just about big gestures and actions. Your meaning is just as useful if you call it to mind to help with the more mundane decision points you encounter daily. The next time you find yourself stuck in a decision, even a minor one, try turning to your meaning to see if this makes it clearer what you want to do. See if it encourages you to behave in ways that are kinder to yourself and others than you might otherwise be, or to be more productive.

Of course, you aren't helping others only to make yourself feel good, you also know it's the right thing to do. But this feedback loop is pretty interesting. When I try to explain how this works to kids, I usually start by having them tell me that I'm stupid. They tend to look at me strangely. I explain that I really do want them to call me stupid, and I go further to tell them that I'm really not worried about being stupid. I deliberate choose that insult, because I feel okay about it. I wouldn't ask them to say something that I was touchy about (like how my stomach pouched in the pants I was wearing), but stupid is fine for me.

Eventually they say, "Elisa, you're stupid." I respond quickly and with emotion, and I say, "No, actually *you're* stupid!" They often jerk back a little (I'm usually pretty nice), and I immediately ask, "Did that make you want to come back at me? To insult me a little more?" They usually say yes. And of course they do. If I'm being rude to them, it makes them want to be mean back to me. I can influence their response to me by how rude I am to them.

But this works both ways. So while I can make you mad at me, I can also make you feel more kind or generous toward me by practicing those traits on you. This isn't done to be manipulative; it's done to create a positive feedback loop between us, where we both like and enjoy each other, and to keep our relationship positive and affirming rather than negative. These prosocial behaviors (respect, listening, kindness) are usually (and usually, unfortunately, does not mean 100 percent every time) reflected back to me. This makes our ability to engage feel more positive and safer, and allows us to connect on a deeper level.

BRAIN HACK: Find five small ways to help others today.

This can be as simple as opening the door for someone, helping your dad put away the groceries, or noticing and complimenting a peer. Notice how your mood feels after you help this person. Did it lighten? If you were feeling bad before, did helping someone help you feel better? One of the coolest things about this hack is how well-grounded it is in research. There is probably an evolutionary reason that we're wired to want to help others—the whole survival-of-the-species idea—but it has been repeatedly shown that kind acts toward others make us and others feel better, so it's clear there are psychological, social, and ethical benefits to complement the evolutionary ones. This is a hack I routinely do, and it always gives me a little boost.

Meaning and happiness are related, but they're not the same thing. Meaning, as you know, is using your strengths in service something greater than yourself. Happiness tends to be more focused on immediate pleasure in the moment. If I were going to think of this visually, I would see happiness as a butterfly—fragile and often in movement, and meaning as the bed of flowers—requiring tending, but more stable and always growing.

Emily Esfahani Smith, a positive psychology researcher who studies this idea, has found that people who report being happy tend to be more self-focused. Their happiness is an experience of comfort and ease, much more about feeling good in the moment. People who report high levels of meaning in their life tend to feel connected to something greater than themselves and are interested in building and strengthening themselves (Smith 2017).

This idea was explored in a study by Roy Baumeister, a psychologist at the University of Florida. In his study, Dr. Baumeister had two groups of college students. One group was assigned the task of doing something that made them happy every day (for example, sleeping late, playing games, shopping, eating sweets), and one group was assigned the task of doing something meaningful every day (for example, forgiving a friend, studying, helping someone). At the end of the study, the happiness people did feel happier. The meaning people did not feel happier, but they did feel a sense of meaning in their lives. Fast-forward three months, and the happiness people no longer felt happier, but the meaning people felt even more enriched, inspired, and like they were a part of something bigger than themselves (Baumeister et al. 2013).

So it really comes down to this: which are you more interested in? Happiness or meaning? Happiness feels good, but it is fleeting. Meaning also feels good (mostly), and it has greater permanence. When we work toward something we believe in, we tend to feel better about ourselves and the world.

But we also want to feel good now. And your brain, at this moment, feels things so intensely that feeling good actually means feeling awesome.

This brings us to another element of the equation, one that makes it easier to stick with the pursuit of meaning, which can be hard, and resist the temptation for easy happiness: purpose.

PURPOSE IS THE PLAN

Purpose describes our intention to do something that we find meaningful, and it also has an impact outside of and beyond ourselves. Meaning is the personal part—what makes you feel something— and purpose is the organizing plan for living a life with meaning. This can be confusing at first, so here are a couple of examples:

Meaning: Painting allows me to express myself and feel joy.

Purpose: My paintings bring beauty to share with others.

Meaning: Studying lets me learn new things.

Purpose: My studying lets me learn all that I will need to know to be a teacher in the future.

Meaning: Talking and connecting with friends makes me feel alive and engaged.

Purpose: I want to find a job where I can connect with others in a way that helps them make their lives better.

What came to mind when you read these examples of meaning and purpose? They may fit with some meaning you have, or they may be examples that have absolutely no personal meaning to you. Either way, that's okay. What does bring you a sense of meaning? It doesn't have to be one thing; it can be many things. In fact, as a teen, your brain is so engaged and connected that you do probably find meaning in multiple areas. That's a good thing. Write down all the things that you think of regarding your meaning, and then take a minute to think about a broader purpose that can relate to your meaning. It can help to think about meaning as the activities or qualities that makes you feel alive and fulfilled, and purpose as the practical way you'll translate those general activities and qualities to concrete tasks or missions in your life.

For instance, if being a vegan is meaningful to you, you might translate that into a purpose like defending animals and fighting against their mal-treatment. In this exercise, writing down a possible purpose is not a com-mitment to do that thing; rather it's a beginning step to clarify your thinking and your beliefs. Don't worry about locking yourself into a life pattern, just brainstorm. No commitment; just exploring. Your meaning and purpose may very well change over time, but let's figure out what drives you right now. As we've discussed, meaning and purpose can improve your mood, motivation, and overall quality of life. Let's try to hack into those strengths by identifying the meaning that drives you right now.

BUILDING YOUR MEANING AND PURPOSE INTO A NARRATIVE

Take a look at the following quote from Ralph Waldo Emerson (an American writer, poet, and naturalist): "The purpose of life is not to be happy. It is to be useful, to be honorable, to be compassionate, to have it make some difference that you have lived and lived well."

Why Am I Doing All This? Finding Meaning

What goes through your mind when you read those lines? If you're like most people, the quote probably makes sense and fits with your beliefs. And now it starts to get trickier. What are you doing to have your life make some difference? This is something I ask myself too. For whatever reason, we humans are very good at continuing along a mundane, day-to-day path without stopping to look around and ask ourselves where we're going and what we're seeing along the way.

We know meaning and purpose matter. We know our brains are designed to find meaning and act with purpose, and yet we often lose track or just forget to focus on these areas. It's a bummer that we do that, because teens (and adults) who have a clear sense of purpose do better; they feel better, they work better, and they value relationships more. But just because we have this tendency to step away from purpose, or to intend to work toward something but then forget about it, doesn't mean it has to be this way. In fact, there are many ways we can change this pattern. One of the most powerful ways to keep purpose in mind is to tell the story of ourselves in a way that includes purpose. The next and final chapter is all about creating your own narrative, the story of you, and how you tell it is up to you. It's a powerful way to build purpose and meaning in your life. Your story is a fitting conclusion for this book. The book ends, but your story is deeply alive.

153

CHAPTER 11

Telling Your Story

I applied to only one graduate school. Looking back, it was a pretty dumb move, and I was lucky I was accepted. But I wasn't surprised that I got in. Not because I was such a great candidate, but because the personal essay I submitted had a line that I considered (and, honestly, still consider) to be powerful. I can't remember what the actual essay was about, but I remember concluding by relaying a conversation with a friend who had asked me what the meaning to life was. I wrote that, of course, the meaning to life was living. I got in, and to this day I credit that line.

Since my kids were little, I have told them that the reason we're here on this earth is to help other people. That, I guess, is my purpose. But my meaning is to live. It's remarkably easy to exist, to repeat patterns, to do the same things, to relax every evening in front of the TV, but what does it mean to really live? To exist in a way in which we experience meaning, purpose, pain, and joy. Being alive and living are different things, and we have choices about which one we adopt. Do we just live or are we actually alive? Part of the way we make the choices about how we want to live is through our narratives.

Your narrative is the story you tell yourself about your life. There can be many meanings given to the same situation. How you perceive an experience is subjective, which means you can choose to tell a story to help or to hurt you. I know a teen, Rebecca, who was bullied every single day during middle school. She literally ate lunch in the bathroom to avoid being teased, and she dreaded going to school each morning. She went home from school and straight to her room, immersed herself in videos, and reemerged only briefly for meals. She was quiet, disconnected from her family, and overwhelmingly sad. Her thoughts focused on how terrible her life, how much she hated herself, and that she was sure her future was destined to be awful.

Her family noticed something was going on, and even though she didn't share what it was, they acted. Her parents signed her up for a summer camp focused on the outdoors. In the camp, kids learned simple survival techniques and an appreciation for nature. Rebecca was not excited, and she was not grateful for the opportunity. But she went, and she made it a life-changing experience for herself. She became physically stronger over the summer, and that change felt powerful. The kids at the camp didn't relate to her the same way that the kids at school did; they didn't have preconceived ideas about who she was and how to act around her. This freedom from a limiting past narrative allowed Rebecca to realize that she could make friends, and that she wasn't damaged or defective as she had previously believed.

Rebecca's favorite part of the camp was the campfire, and this is where stories were told. One of the stories was the tale of the phoenix, a bird that could be born again. The phoenix would burst into flames and then, from the flames, would emerge a new bird with greater powers. This story resonated for Rebecca, this idea of rebirth and re-creation, and she made the story part of her own narrative. She would re-create herself. She would still be Rebecca, but she wouldn't be the Rebecca who hid. She would be Rebecca who stood strong in plain sight.

Rebecca began to craft a new narrative about herself, and her new story reframed her past experiences and used that summer as a time of re-creation. Rebecca's story was about her struggle: She didn't pretend that the mistreatment by her peers hadn't happened, and she didn't rewrite the story to soften their guilt or minimize the pain she had experienced. Instead, she retold her narrative as a survivor. As someone who had been through a terrible ordeal and risen from its ashes to be herself again. She thought of herself as the phoenix. Kids at school had tried to make her believe that she was nothing, but she was actually capable of rebirth from the flames and the pain around her. She was a strong person who had endured unfairness. She was far tougher than most kids her age, and now she was also far stronger. She would rise again.

Stories are one of the oldest traditions of humans. As long as we have had language, there have been stories, and there is reason for that. Stories are for sharing information, for learning, and for providing motivation, meaning, and purpose. Our brains remember information better in story form, and the emotion the stories elicit provides motivation and change. Let's look more closely at how this works in the brain.

MIRROR NEURONS AND STORIES

Mirror neurons are—guess what?—neurons that mirror another person's experience. The name actually makes sense. These neurons are in our frontal lobes, and they go off when we see someone else having an experience. These neurons lead us to feel empathy and compassion for each other. We can even feel, to some degree, the pain of another person through these neurons.

A researcher named Giacomo Rizzolatti and his colleagues first identified mirror neurons in monkeys. Monkeys were hooked up to devices that measured activity in a specific region of their brain called the ventral motor cortex. The researchers were interested in understanding how the neurons activated as the monkeys used their hands and feet to move objects. The team discovered that when monkeys picked up food, certain neurons activated, and—and this is the interesting part—when the researchers picked up their own food, the same neurons activated again in the monkeys' brains. They monkeys' brains reacted similarly to their own food and to someone else's food. These neurons were called mirror neurons as they seemed to mirror the same place in the brain for both the act of eating and the act of watching someone else eat (Rizzolatti et al 1996).

The study with monkeys was many years ago, and since that time much more has been learned about mirror neurons. The research on these neurons continues to grow and evolve, but recent studies have seen their role in stories.

Transportation is a word with a special meaning in the realm of stories. It's the official term for the experience of feeling like we're in the story. Technically, transportation occurs when our attention and anxiety come together with empathy. Cortisol releases, heightening our attention; and oxytocin releases, making us feel more caring and connected to the story. We "transport" into the story itself, and our brains continue to respond with chemical releases and activating neurons. Our mirror neurons respond to shared experience, to pain, and to joy (Smith 2016).

YOUR NARRATIVE BRAIN

King Henry died drinking chocolate milk. It's not an eloquent story, it's just a sentence, but even as I write it I have an image of a king lying face-down on a golden table next to his goblet of chocolate milk. Of course, there is no such King Henry, and even if there were, it's doubtful that he would have drunk much chocolate milk, but I still remember that sentence from many decades ago. I had to Google what it actually stood for (it's a mnemonic, a memory device for the metric prefixes kilo, hecto, deca, deci, centi, and milli), but I remember it because it gave a sense of story.

We are wired for stories. Researchers have found that we remember things better in story form. We engage with others more over stories. We even have a greater oxytocin response to stories than we do to information presented in nonstory form (Zak 2014). Stories elicit emotion, they engage us, and they create an alternate path and meaning. Rebecca is hardly the first person to be inspired by a story; I imagine it would be hard to find someone who hasn't been changed by a story.

What's your favorite story? The one you listened to over and over? The one that made you feel strong and powerful or calm and safe? If you can't remember, ask the person who used to read you bedtime stories. There's a good chance they still remember your favorite stories; kids like repetition, and they probably read it to you over and over and over.

Additionally, stories teach us how to solve problems and learn from others; there is an evolutionary reason our brain hangs on so tightly to stories. In fact, one study looked at the ability of people to read another person's perspective, to essentially see the world through their eyes. The participants who read "high quality" fiction were better able to recognize emotional states in pictures of people's eyes than the participants who did not read the stories. The story-reading primed their brain to better read emotion (Comer and Castan 2013).

Stories are an essential part of being human, and we use them to learn and to grow. And just as we can learn and empathize with characters in a story we hear or read, we also can learn and grow from the stories we build about ourselves. We get to decide who we are in the world, and we get to find ways to either boost ourselves up with our words and thoughts or knock ourselves down.

STORY + MEANING = ACTION

I just made up that equation, but it makes sense. If we combine our meaning with our story, we activate our limbic system, we activate our PFC, and our whole brain is engaged in working together to create something meaningful to move us forward. This is where CBT is essential. It's too easy to craft a story of convenience, of victimhood, and of defeat. That story isn't going to motivate you, it's going to keep you stuck in patterns and unable to move forward.

Neil Gaiman (2015), the master of myth and story, wrote in his novel *Coraline:* "Fairy tales are more than true: not because they tell us that dragons exist, but because they tell us that dragons can be beaten." We can change our thoughts, we can reframe our experiences, and we can build narratives that let us slay our own dragons.

Here's a more practical example, no real or metaphoric dragons involved. Dr. Xiaodong Lin-Siegler and several colleagues did a study on the power of story with four hundred ninth and tenth graders at low-income schools in New York City. Many of these students had an internal narrative that success came from natural ability. And since they didn't see themselves as naturally gifted, they didn't think they had a chance at success.

To see if they could challenge students' beliefs, the researchers had one group of students read stories about famous scientists like Albert Einstein and Marie Curie. The stories showed the struggles the scientists faced, and how they overcame them through perseverance, advocacy, or asking for help. The stories showed that these eminent scientists were just people who had overcome adversity and struggle to reach their success. After six weeks, the teens who had read about the scientists' struggles were significantly more likely to improve their science learning . The teens in this group were more willing to believe that they could be successful through effort and hard work, rather than, as they had originally thought, having to be innately skilled in these areas. The group that did not read about the struggles of the scientists maintained the same beliefs that they started with; that only those with inborn talents could succeed (Lin-Siegler et al. 2016).

The stories changed the students' beliefs. Your story can change your beliefs. And your story can be written today, right now, and in a way that reflects who you are and who you want to be. Creating your own narrative is an act of power, and it lets you decide how you want to live in the world. When we don't actively choose to tell our own story, we often default to the easiest explanations. No surprise here, but those explanations are often of being a victim, less-than or not-enough. Choose differently. As you think about your own narrative, take a minute to write down some ideas about how you want to see yourself. Remember, there is a difference between just living and being alive; your story can be a map to help you fully live.

Conclusion:
Your Path Forward

You now have an owner's manual to your brain that is full of research-based CBT strategies to help you navigate your path forward. Your path is influenced by this stage of your brain, but it still is your path. You have an understanding of the unique challenges of being an adolescent, and hopefully you also have an understanding of the awesome (true definition: being marked by awe) abilities of your teen brain. You can learn more, feel more, and do more than at any other time in your life before.

Yes, there are costs to this power. Your brain is constantly seeking reward, and it loves to feel good. The wiring is not fully complete, and this presents some problems as emotions become amplified when they can't connect to the PFC. But you know this now, and you can do things about it. You can use your thoughts when you realize your emotions are surging. You can choose to just feel, or you can choose to change and manage your emotions. It's like you're in control of a beautiful car with crazy-fast acceleration but slightly lagging brakes. If you know how to use the brakes, understand their quirks and their limitations, then you can still drive the way you want to drive.

Feelings, friends, stress, learning, chilling, meaning—all this is doable, because you understand the dynamics of yourself, of the age, and of others.

And you now get to craft your story moving forward. It doesn't have to be about the you that you were, but it does need to be about the you that you want to be.

Acknowledgments

It is with gratitude that I acknowledge the efforts of the New Harbinger team in helping this book come together. Jess O'Brien, my acquisitions editor, helped shape the idea of this book and advocated for its creation. He is patient, full of good will, humor, and consistent encouragement. Vicraj Gill is a detailed and thoughtful editor who can organize and make sense of almost anything. Copy editor Karen Schader misses nothing and questions gently. Karen is a true support and she makes my writing better.

References

Achor, S. 2010. *The Happiness Advantage: The Seven Principles of Positive Psychology That Fuel Success and Performance at Work.* New York: Crown Business.

Allen, D. 2015. *Getting Things Done: How to Achieve Stress-Free Productivity.* New York: Penguin.

Allen, J., J. Chango, D. Szwedo, M. Schad, and E. Marston. 2012. "Predictors of Susceptibility to Peer Influence Regarding Substance Use in Adolescence." *Child Development* 83(1): 337–350.

Baudry, M., X. Bi, C. Gall, and G. Lynch. 2011. "The Biochemistry of Memory: The Twenty-Six Year Journey of a 'New and Specific Hypothesis'." *Neurobiology of Learning and Memory* 95(2): 125–133.

Baumeister, R. F., K. D. Vohs, J. L. Aaker, and E. N. Garbinsky. 2013. "Some Key Differences Between a Happy Life and a Meaningful Life." *Journal of Positive Psychology* 8(6): 505–516.

Bjork, E. L., and R. A. Bjork. 2014. "Making Things Hard on Yourself, But in a Good Way: Creating Desirable Difficulties to Enhance Learning." In *Psychology and the Real World: Essays Illustrating Fundamental Contributions to Society,* edited by M. A. Gernsbacher and J. R. Pomerantz. 2nd ed. New York: Worth Publishers.

Blakemore, S-J. 2018. *Inventing Ourselves: The Secret Life of the Teenage Brain.* 1st ed. New York: PublicAffairs.

Blakemore, S-J., and K. L. Mills. 2014. "Is Adolescence a Sensitive Period for Sociocultural Processing?" *Annual Review of Psychology* 65(1): 187–207.

Bower, G. H. 1981. "Mood and Memory." *American Psychologist* 36(2): 129–148.

Bronk, K. C. 2014. *Purpose in Life.* Place of publication not identified: Springer.

Burnett, D. 2018. *Happy Brain: Where Happiness Comes From, and Why.* New York: W.W. Norton and Company.

Carey, B. 2015. *How We Learn: The Surprising Truth About When, Where, and Why It Happens.* New York: Random House.

Centers for Disease Control and Prevention (CDC). 2020. "Keep Teen Drivers Safe." October 23. https://www.cdc.gov/injury/features/teen-drivers/index.html.

Comer Kidd, D., and E. Castano. 2013. "Reading Literary Fiction Improves Theory of Mind." *Science,* 342(6156): 377–380.

Crum, A. J., P. Salovey, and S. Achor. 2013. "Rethinking Stress: The Role of Mindsets in Determining the Stress Response." *Journal of Personality and Social Psychology* 104(4): 716–733.

Dahl, C. J., C. H. Wilson-Mendenhall, and R. J. Davidson, (2020). "The Plasticity of Well-Being: A Training-Based Framework for the Cultivation of Human Flourishing." *Proceedings of the National*

Academy of Sciences of the United States of America 117(51): 32197–32206.

Fenesi, B., K. Lucibello, J. A. Kim, and J. J. Heisz. 2018. "Sweat So You Don't Forget: Exercise Breaks During a University Lecture Increase On-Task Attention and Learning." *Journal of Applied Research in Memory and Cognition* 7(2): 261–269.

Frankl, V. 2019. *Man's Search for Meaning.* 4th ed. Boston: Beacon Press.

Fredrickson, B. L., K. M. Grewen, K. A. Coffey, S. B. Algoe, A. M. Firestine, J. M. Arevalo, J. Ma, and S. W. Cole. 2013. "A Functional Genomic Perspective on Human Well-Being." *Proceedings of the National Academy of Sciences of the United States of America* 110(33): 13684–13689.

Fredrickson, B. L., and M. F. Losada. 2005. "Positive Affect and the Complex Dynamics of Human Flourishing." *American Psychologist* 60(7): 678–686.

Gaiman, N. 2006. *Coraline.* New York: Harper Perennial.

Gallace, A., D. M. Torta, G. L. Moseley, and G. D. Iannetti. 2011. "The Analgesic Effect of Crossing the Arms." *Pain* 152(6): 1418–1423.

Galván A., and A. Rahdar. 2013. "The Neurobiological Effects of Stress on Adolescent Decision Making." *Neuroscience.* 249: 223–231.

Halamish, V., and R. A. Bjork. 2011. "When Does Testing Enhance Retention? A Distribution-Based Interpretation of Retrieval As a Memory Modifier." *Journal of Experimental Psychology: Learning, Memory, and Cognition* 37(4): 801–812.

Harris, D. 2019. *10% Happier: How I How I Tamed the Voice in My Head, Reduced Stress Without Losing My Edge, and Found Self-Help That Actually Works.* New York: Dey Street Books.

Hull, C. L. 1938. "The Goal-Gradient Hypothesis Applied to Some 'Field-Force' Problems in the Behavior of Young Children." *Psychological Review* 45(4): 271–299.

Inagaki, T. K., H. K. E. Bryne, S. Suzuki, I. Jevtic, E. Hornstein, J. E. Bower, and N. I. Eisenberger. 2016. "The Neurobiology of Giving Versus Receiving Support: The Role of Stress-Related and Social Reward-Related Neural Activity." *Psychosomatic Medicine* 78(4): 443–453.

Isen, A. M., K. A. Daubman, and G. P. Nowicki. 1987. "Positive Affect Facilitates Creative Problem Solving." *Journal of Personality and Social Psychology* 52 (June), 1122–1131.

Jamieson, J. P., M. K. Nock, and W. B. Mendes. 2012. "Mind Over Matter: Reappraising Arousal Improves Cardiovascular and Cognitive Responses to Stress." *Journal of Experimental Psychology* 141(3): 417–422.

Jensen, F., and A. E. Nutt. 2015. *The Teenage Brain: A Neuroscientist's Survival Guide to Raising Adolescents and Young Adults.* 1st ed. New York: Harper.

Keller, A., K. Litzelman, L. E. Wisk, T. Maddox, E. R. Cheng, P. D. Creswell, and W. P. Witt. 2012. "Does the Perception That Stress Affects Health Matter? The Association with Health and Mortality." *Health Psychology* 31(5): 677–684.

Killingsworth, M., and D. Gilbert. 2010. "A Wandering Mind Is an Unhappy Mind." *Science,* 330(6006): 932.

Kim, E. S., S. D. Hershner, and V. J. Strecher. 2015. "Purpose in Life and Incidence of Sleep Disturbances." *Journal of Behavioral Medicine* 38(3): 590–597.

Kircanski, K., M. D. Lieberman, and M.G. Craske. 2012. "Feelings Into Words: Contributions of Language to Exposure Therapy." *Psychological Science* 23 (10): 1086–1091.

Konnikova, M. 2014. "Getting Over Procrastination." *New Yorker,* July 22.

Kornell, N., and R. A. Bjork. 2008. "Learning Concepts and Categories: Is Spacing the 'Enemy of Induction'?" *Psychological Science* 19(6): 585–592.

Kross, E., E. Bruehlman-Senecal, J. Park, A. Burson, A. Dougherty, H. Shablac, A. Bremner, and O. Ayduk. 2014. "Self-Talk as a Regulatory Mechanism: How You Do It Matters." *Journal of Personality and Social Psychology* 106(2): 304–324.

Lees, B., L. R. Meredith, B. E. Bryant, and L. M. Squeglia. 2020. "Effect of Alcohol Use on the Adolescent Brain and Behavior." *Pharmacology Biochemistry and Behavior* 192.

Lieberman, C. 2019. "Why You Procrastinate (It Has Nothing to Do with Self-Control)." *New York Times,* March 25.

Lin-Siegler, X., J. N. Ahn, J. Chen, F-F. A. Fang, and M. Luna-Lucerno. 2016. "Even Einstein Struggled: Effects of Learning About Great Scientists' Struggles on High School Students' Motivation to Learn Science." *Journal of Educational Psychology* 108(3): 314–328.

Lueke, A., and B. Gibson. 2014. "Mindfulness Meditation Reduces Implicit Age and Race Bias: The Role of Reduced Automaticity of Responding." *Social Psychology and Personality Science* 6(3): 284–291.

Mednick, S. C., and M. Ehrman. 2006. *Take a Nap! Change Your Life: The Scientific Plan to Make You Smarter, Healthier, More Productive.* New York: Workman.

McGonigal, K. 2015. *The Upside of Stress: Why Stress Is Good for You, and How to Get Good at It.* New York: Avery.

Nozick, R. 1974. *Anarchy, State, and Utopia.* New York: Basic Books.

Ramsden, S., F. M. Richardson, G. Josse, M. S. C. Thomas, C. Ellis, C. Shakeshaft, M. L. Seghier, and C. J. Price. 2011. "Verbal and Non-Verbal Intelligence Changes in the Teenage Brain." *Nature* 479(7371): 113–116.

Reyna, V. F., S. M. Estrada, R. M. DeMarinis, J. M. Stanisz, and B. A. Mills. 2011. "Neurobiological and Memory Models of Risky Decision Making in Adolescents Versus Young Adults." *Journal of Experimental Social Psychology* 37(5): 1125–1142.

Rizzolatti, G., L. Fadiga, V. Gallese, and L. Fogassi (1996). "Premotor Cortex and the Recognition of Motor Actions." *Cognitive Brain Research* 3(2): 131–141.

Sanger, K. L., and Dorjee, D. (2015). "Mindfulness Training for Adolescents: A Neurodevelopmental Perspective on Investigating Modifications in Attention and Emotion Regulation Using Event-Related Brain Potentials." *Cognitive, Affective and Behavioral Neuroscience* 15(3): 696–711.

Savage, B. M., H. L. Lujan, R. R. Thipparthi, and S. E. DiCarlo. 2017. "Humor, Laughter, Learning, and Health! A Brief Review." *Advances in Physiology Education* 41(3): 341–347.

Shellenbarger, S. 2016. "What Teens Need Most from Their Parents." *Wall Street Journal,* August 10.

Siegel, D. J. 2013. *Brainstorm: The Power and Purpose of the Teenage Brain.* New York: Jeremy P. Tarcher/Penguin.

Sirois, F., and T. Pychyl. 2013. "Procrastination and the Priority of Short-Term Mood Regulation: Consequences for Future Self." *Social and Personality Psychology Compass* 7(2): 115–127.

Smith, E. E. 2017. *The Power of Meaning: Finding Fulfillment in a World Obsessed with Happiness.* New York: Broadway Books.

Smith, J. 2016. "The Science of the Story." *Berkeley News,* August 25.

Smith, S.M., A. Glenberg, and R. A. Bjork.1978. "Environmental Context and Human Memory." *Memory and Cognition* 6: 342–353.

Steel, P. 2011. *The Procrastination Equation: How to Stop Putting Things Off and Start Getting Stuff Done.* 1st ed. New York: Harper.

Steinberg, L. (2013, February 8). *A Social Neuroscience Perspective on Adolescent Risk Taking.* https://www.cornell.edu/video/social-neuroscience-perspective-adolescent-risk-taking

Steinberg, L. 2014. *Age of Opportunity.* New York: Houghton Mifflin Harcourt.

Taylor, J. B. 2006. *My Stroke of Insight: A Brain Scientist's Personal Journey.* New York: Penguin.

Telzer, E. H., Y. Ichien, and Y. Qu. 2015. "Mothers Know Best: Redirecting Adolescent Reward Sensitivity Toward Safe Behavior During Risk Taking." *Social Cognitive and Affective Neuroscience* 10(10): 1383–1391.

Torres, J. B., and M. D. Lieberman. 2018. "Putting Feelings into Words: Affect Labeling as Implicit Emotion Regulation." *Emotion Review* 10(2): 116–124.

Tseng, J., and J. Poppenk. 2020. "Brain Meta-State Transitions Demarcate Thoughts Across Task Contexts Exposing the Mental Noise of Trait Neuroticism." *Nature Communications* 11, 3480.

Way, N. 2013. "Boys' Friendships During Adolescence: Intimacy, Desire, and Loss." *Journal of Research on Adolescence* 23(2): 201–213.

Yuan, J. P., C. G. Connolly, E. Henje, L. P. Sugrue, T. T. Yang, D. Xu, and O. Tymofiyeva. 2020. "Gray Matter Changes in Adolescents Participating in a Meditation Training." *Frontiers in Human Neuroscience* 14:319.

Zak, P. J. 2014. "Why Your Brain Loves Good Storytelling." October 24. https://hbr.org/2014/10/why-your-brain-loves-good-storytelling

Elisa Nebolsine, LCSW, is owner and clinician at CBT for Kids, a private practice in Alexandria, VA. She is adjunct faculty at the Beck Institute for Cognitive Behavior Therapy, adjunct faculty at the Catholic University of America, and a diplomate of the Academy of Cognitive Therapy. She has presented locally and nationally on the topic of cognitive behavioral therapy (CBT), and is a consultant for schools, agencies, and other organizations on the implementation and use of CBT with children, teens, and young adults. She is author of *The Grit Workbook for Kids*.

Foreword writer **Judith S. Beck, PhD,** is president of the Beck Institute for Cognitive Behavior Therapy and clinical professor of psychology in psychiatry at the University of Pennsylvania. She is author of the seminal text, *Cognitive Therapy*, which has been translated into more than twenty languages, and whose third edition contains a recovery orientation.

Real change *is* possible

For more than forty-five years, New Harbinger has published proven-effective self-help books and pioneering workbooks to help readers of all ages and backgrounds improve mental health and well-being, and achieve lasting personal growth. In addition, our spirituality books offer profound guidance for deepening awareness and cultivating healing, self-discovery, and fulfillment.

Founded by psychologist Matthew McKay and Patrick Fanning, New Harbinger is proud to be an independent, employee-owned company. Our books reflect our core values of integrity, innovation, commitment, sustainability, compassion, and trust. Written by leaders in the field and recommended by therapists worldwide, New Harbinger books are practical, accessible, and provide real tools for real change.

 newharbingerpublications

More ⏱Instant Help Books for Teens

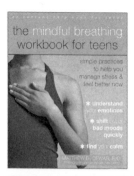

THE MINDFUL BREATHING WORKBOOK FOR TEENS

Simple Practices to Help You Manage Stress and Feel Better Now

978-1-684037247 / US $17.95

THE GROWTH MINDSET WORKBOOK FOR TEENS

Say Yes to Challenges, Deal with Difficult Emotions, and Reach Your Full Potential

978-1684035571 / US $18.95

THE TEEN GIRL'S SURVIVAL GUIDE

Ten Tips for Making Friends, Avoiding Drama, and Coping with Social Stress

978-1626253063 / US $17.95

THE RESILIENT TEEN

10 Key Skills to Bounce Back from Setbacks and Turn Stress into Success

978-1684035786 / US $17.95

CONQUER NEGATIVE THINKING FOR TEENS

A Workbook to Break the Nine Thought Habits That Are Holding You Back

978-1626258891 / US $17.95

PUT YOUR WORRIES HERE

A Creative Journal for Teens with Anxiety

978-1684032143 / US $17.95

🌱 **newharbinger**publications

1-800-748-6273 / newharbinger.com

(VISA, MC, AMEX / prices subject to change without notice)
Follow Us 📷 📘 🐦 📹 📌 in

Don't miss out on new books in the subjects that interest you.
Sign up for our Book Alerts at **newharbinger.com/bookalerts** ✎